ASK GRANDPA

*To John & Donna
with love
Bud*

ASK GRANDPA
53 Reflections On Life From An Old Man

CHARLES "BUD" VEAR

Copyright © 2020 by Charles "Bud" Vear.

ISBN:	Softcover	978-1-7960-8278-4
	eBook	978-1-7960-8277-7

All rights reserved. No part of this book may be reproduced or transmitted in any form or by any means, electronic or mechanical, including photocopying, recording, or by any information storage and retrieval system, without permission in writing from the copyright owner.

Any people depicted in stock imagery provided by Getty Images are models, and such images are being used for illustrative purposes only.
Certain stock imagery © Getty Images.

Print information available on the last page.

Rev. date: 01/24/2020

To order additional copies of this book, contact:
Xlibris
1-888-795-4274
www.Xlibris.com
Orders@Xlibris.com
808306

DEDICATION

This book is dedicated to my wife, Gloria, who was my partner and my optimistic visionary for 68 years. We shared many of the experiences I refer to in these reflections, and she provided me with encouragement and advice when these were appropriate. My life was a positive and exciting adventure because of her. She is gone now, but her inspiration continues. I also acknowledge the important role our children and grandchildren have played in impacting our lives and enriching life's meaning. Our roles are reversing, but the importance of a loving family is enhanced by this change.

CONTENTS

Dedication v
Preface ix

Abortion 1
Aging 3
America 7
Apologies 10
Big City Life 12
Canoeing & Rafting 15
Careers 19
Cars 22
Charity 25
Children 28
Choices 32
Communes 34
Death Penalty 37
Faith 40
Family Vacations 42
Favorite Child 46
Free Enterprise 48
Gambling 50
Generosity 53
Goodness 56
Immigration 59
Important People 62
Killing 66
Leadership 68

Life	71
Longevity	73
Love	76
Marriage	78
Medicine	82
Money	85
Morality	88
Opinions	91
Personality Flaws	94
Planned Parenthood	97
Popularity	99
Prejudice	101
Pro-Life	104
Protests	107
Rich & Poor	110
Saving	113
School	116
Servant Heart	119
Sports	122
Summer Camp	126
Summer Vacations	129
Theatre	134
The Olden Days	140
Tolerance	143
Volunteering	147
War	149
Weather	151
When a Loved One Dies	153
World War II	155

PREFACE

Old people, having lived through many life experiences, often like to share the wisdom they have gained – especially with their grandchildren. Part of this is storytelling, but part is a desire to help younger people avoid some of the mistakes we oldsters have made.   (Unfortunately, most of us learn from our own mistakes and not from the mistakes of others.)

The "Ask Grandpa" reflections in the following pages are examples of the wisdom gained from living a long time. You may not agree with everything in these reflections, but, hopefully, they will cause you to ponder a bit. Take from them what you wish. I hope you will enjoy my reflections from my journey through life.

Grandpa Doc

ABORTION

Grandchild: Grandpa, you don't like abortion do you?
Grandpa: Do you?
Grandchild: Only when it's necessary.
Grandpa: And when is it necessary?
Grandchild: I guess it's when the woman decides it's necessary.
Grandpa: What would make her decide to have an abortion?
Grandchild: Maybe she doesn't have enough money to raise a child.
Grandpa: So, it's an economic decision then. A child is only welcome if it fits into your budget.
Grandchild: That's not what I meant. Maybe she did not want to get pregnant.
Grandpa: You do know how pregnancy occurs, don't you?
Grandchild: Of course I do. You don't have to explain the birds and the bees to me. Sometimes people get pregnant when they don't want to. Shouldn't they be able to decide whether they should continue the pregnancy?
Grandpa: Does the baby have a vote on this?
Grandchild: Not really.
Grandpa: So, the mother decides whether her baby lives or dies.
Grandchild: I guess so, but the unborn baby is not able to make decisions.
Grandpa: Kind of like a two year old.
Grandchild: What do you mean?

Grandpa:	A two year old can't make decisions either. That's why it needs parents.
Grandchild:	What does that have to do with an unborn baby?
Grandpa:	Well, if your justification for killing an unborn child is lack of money or the child's inability to make decisions, then the same choice could be made for a two year old.
Grandchild:	But the two year old is already born.
Grandpa:	The only differences between the two is their age and their locations. They are both human beings. If you can justify killing one, then you can justify killing the other.
Grandchild:	But it would be against the law to kill the two year old.
Grandpa:	That's correct.
Grandchild:	And abortion is legal.
Grandpa:	That's also correct – but is it right?
Grandchild:	What do you mean?
Grandpa:	Owning slaves was legal, but was it right?
Grandchild:	Of course not. We had a Civil War to decide that.
Grandpa:	Then maybe abortion is legal but not right.
Grandchild:	You have a point. Maybe I need to do some more thinking about abortion.
Grandpa:	Probably a good idea. Just remember that the primary purpose of an abortion is to kill the unborn child. A failed abortion is when the baby lives.
Grandchild:	That's pretty graphic.
Grandpa:	But isn't that the truth?
Grandchild:	OK, I guess you're right. Why do you have to be so logical? Thanks, Grandpa

AGING

Grandchild: Grandpa, how did you get to be so old?
Grandpa: Are you complaining?
Grandchild: Oh no! I want to keep you around. I just wondered how you and Grandma managed to live so long.
Grandpa: We picked our parents very carefully.
Grandchild: Aw come on, Grandpa; you can't pick your parents.
Grandpa: You're right, but if you want to live a long life, it helps to have ancestors who lived to an old age. Your Grandma's mother lived to be almost 87, and my Father was 91 when he died.
Grandchild: That means that you have both lived longer than one of your parents.
Grandpa: Just barely.
Grandchild: What about your mother and Grandma's father?
Grandpa: Both died of unnatural causes, not from old age. My mother died at 61 because of a surgical complication and your Grandma's father died quite young when he was in the Army and decided to dry clean his clothes with gasoline, and his clothes caught fire. Neither lived as long as they normally would have.
Grandchild: You outlived all three of your brothers, so your ancestors' longevity didn't seem to help them as much. How come?

Grandpa:	While ancestry is important, lifestyle choices also play a part in how long you live. You can't choose your ancestry, but you do choose your lifestyle.
Grandchild:	So what did you do differently than your brothers?
Grandpa:	First of all, I didn't smoke. Two of my brothers were heavy smokers. One of my brothers was a heavy drinker, and I never drank very much. I also have tried to exercise regularly all my life, but so did one of my brothers, who died at 74. In addition to lifestyle choices, there are health issues that develop over which we don't have much control. My exercising brother developed Parkinson Disease in his later years and ended up dying of cancer. Another brother died of Pneumonia and the third died suddenly of a ruptured aneurysm, so probably none of their deaths were related to lifestyle choices. That doesn't mean that lifestyle choices are not important. It simply means that, in spite of living a healthy life and having good genetics we are all subject to life ending conditions over which we have little control.
Grandchild:	I guess I should be thankful that I have good genetics.
Grandpa:	Try not to mess them up. My father's family tree now contains over 250 branches. Only two people in that tree, below my generation have died.
Grandchild:	How long do you want to live, Grandpa?
Grandpa:	I guess the best answer is, "as long as God's thinks I can be useful down here."
Grandchild:	What deficiencies have you noticed most about growing old?
Grandpa:	There are three things that I have lost in the aging process.
Grandchild:	And what are those"
Grandpa:	I have noticed loss of strength and loss of balance.
Grandchild:	What is the third?
Grandpa:	I can't remember.
Grandchild:	You're funny, Grandpa. You and Grandma seem happy. Why do you think you have managed to be so happy?

	You have certainly had challenges in your life –especially from your twelve children.
Grandpa:	Happiness is not something you are given. It is something you create. Other people are not responsible for your happiness. I think you can be as happy as you choose to be. There are many examples of happy people who seem to have nothing and unhappy people who seem to have everything. Some people complain their way thru life while others look for the bright side of every situation. Lou Holtz, the very successful Notre Dame Football coach, was also a great motivational speaker, and one of his most profound observations was that 90% of people don't want to hear your complaints and the other 10% are glad you have them. So, why complain!
Grandchild:	What are your keys to being happy?
Grandpa:	I have decided that there are four things, in life, that you need for happiness.
Grandchild:	Only four? I can think of a lot more things that would make me feel happy.
Grandpa:	Most of those are probably things that produce short term happiness. I'm talking about the long term keys to happiness.
Grandchild:	I think you are about to deliver your words of wisdom.
Grandpa:	Wisdom is what I possess the most of.
Grandchild:	OK, share your wisdom with me. What are your keys to happiness?
Grandpa:	To be happy, I think most of us need someone to love, something to do and something to look forward to.
Grandchild:	That's only three. What is the fourth?
Grandpa:	Not everyone will agree, but I think that belief in an Almighty and merciful God is necessary to be truly happy. I take comfort in the fact that I'm not in complete control of what happens to me.
Grandchild:	How would you like to be remembered?

Grandpa: I would like to be remembered as someone who has made a difference – that my life has been worthwhile.

Grandchild: I think you and Grandma both qualify on that score, and I hope the Lord doesn't think you are done yet. Thanks, Grandpa

AMERICA

Grandchild: Grandpa, did you ever want to live in another Country?
Grandpa: Why would I want to do that?
Grandchild: Well, I've heard you complain about some of the things that are happening in this Country.
Grandpa: That's true. There are some things that happen here that I don't approve of.
Grandchild: So, where would you like to live?
Grandpa: In the United States.
Grandchild: But I thought you said you were unhappy with some things in this Country?
Grandpa: I did, but I still think it is the best Country in the world.
Grandchild: Why do you say that?
Grandpa: Because it has given me the freedom to pursue my dreams.
Grandchild: Can't you do that in other Countries just as well?
Grandpa: I can't answer that question because I have never lived in another Country, but I do know that I have enjoyed the freedom in this Country to decide what I want to do without having the government control me as I'm told they do in some other Nations.
Grandchild: What about the things you don't like about this Country?
Grandpa: I have the freedom to try to change them or to elect people who will change them. The United States has survived many wars and natural disasters and is still one of the longest surviving democracies the world has ever

	known? That's why so many immigrants want to come here.
Grandchild:	What do you mean by democracy?
Grandpa:	Well, actually we function as a Democratic Republic.
Grandchild:	What's the difference?
Grandpa:	In a pure democracy, all decisions would be made by a vote of all the people. In a Democratic Republic, we are represented by the people we elect. They do the voting and make decisions for us. It is much more efficient than a pure Democracy, and the people are still in charge. If we don't like decisions that our representatives make, we can replace them by voting for someone else.
Grandchild:	Some people say that our Country wants to control the whole world.
Grandpa:	That's an interesting opinion. We helped win two World Wars in other Countries, with the sacrifice of tens of thousands of our soldiers, and we didn't take control of any additional territory after the wars ended. That's hardly an example of conquest.
Grandchild:	So why do you like our Country so much?
Grandpa:	Do you think we are a generous Nation:
Grandchild:	I think you are getting ready to deliver one of your pearls of wisdom.
Grandpa:	No, just a simple question.
Grandchild:	I think I am supposed to say "yes".
Grandpa:	That's the right answer, but I don't think you believe or understand it.
Grandchild:	OK, what's your evidence?
Grandpa:	First of all, our Nation gives millions of dollars in aid to many other Nations. Secondly, we use our military power, often at the cost of American lives, to help other Nations maintain their freedom. And thirdly we Americans voluntarily donate millions of dollars each year to support churches and other organizations in our Country and around the World that provide help for the

	poor and the needy. I doubt that our level of generosity is common in most other Nations.
Grandchild:	What makes you think that?
Grandpa:	Let me give you one example from my own experience. The first time we went to Germany to visit our exchange students, we attended a small church in a very small German town. When the nearly empty collection basket came to me, I decided to be generous and put a little extra German money in the basket. I thought the church must be struggling to support itself with the little the parishioners contributed. Later I found out that the churches in Germany don't depend on parishioner donations. They are supported by a percentage of the taxes that people pay each year to the government. Thus there is no need or incentive for the people in Germany to be generous by making voluntary contributions to the churches they attend. In our Country, on the other hand, the support of churches is completely voluntary, and our churches depend on this voluntary support for their survival.
Grandchild:	So, that makes us a more generous people?
Grandpa:	I think that is the pearl of wisdom you were looking for.
Grandchild:	Not sure I was looking for it, but it came anyway.
Grandpa:	You are now a little wiser.
Grandchild:	Not sure of that, but I think I understand why you like this Country in spite of its shortcomings.
Grandpa:	And remember that living in this Country is a privilege, but also a choice. You can move elsewhere if you don't like it here. There are plenty of eager potential immigrants who would gladly trade places with you.
Grandchild:	No thanks! I think I'll stay here.
Grandpa:	You <u>are</u> getting wiser.
Grandchild:	Thanks, Grandpa.

APOLOGIES

Grandchild: Did you ever have to apologize, Grandpa?
Grandpa: Why do you ask?
Grandchild: Well, I have great difficulty apologizing.
Grandpa: And why is that?
Grandchild: If I apologize, it means I've been wrong, and I don't like to admit that I'm wrong.
Grandpa: What if you <u>are</u> wrong?
Grandchild: Do I have to admit it?
Grandpa: No, but <u>should</u> you admit it?
Grandchild: I think you are going to bring up the Ten Commandments again.
Grandpa: Is that bad?
Grandchild: Not bad. It just usually makes me feel guilty.
Grandpa: Let me ask you a question. If you have done something that harms someone else, how would you feel?
Grandchild: That depends. If they hurt me, I may feel they had it coming.
Grandpa: And what if they come to you and say they are sorry for what they did?
Grandchild: Then I would probably tell them I am sorry, too.
Grandpa: How would those two apologies make you feel toward each other?
Grandchild: I guess it might restore our friendship.
Grandpa: And wouldn't that be a good thing?

Grandchild:	I guess so.
Grandpa:	Now, suppose neither of you apologize. How would you feel then?
Grandchild:	We would probably not want to see each other again.
Grandpa:	And would that be a good thing?
Grandchild:	I suppose not.
Grandpa:	Now, let me pose a more difficult question. Suppose you have had a disagreement with a friend, and you both have suffered hurt feelings. You both think you are right. Your friend doesn't apologize. Would you?
Grandchild:	Even if I was right?
Grandpa:	Even if you were right.
Grandchild:	Why would I apologize if I was right?
Grandpa:	Because you have hurt your friend's feelings.
Grandchild:	You mean I should apologize even if I'm right?
Grandpa:	That's up to you, but what effect do you think your apology would have on your friend?
Grandchild:	I suppose he would be pleased, but wouldn't that be an admission by me that I am wrong?
Grandpa:	Not if you simply apologize for the disagreement and for hurting his feelings. It is possible to disagree and not destroy a relationship.
Grandchild:	Where did you learn all this apology stuff?
Grandpa:	In my marriage. Husbands and wives sometimes have disagreements, but the reason long marriages survive is because both partners learn to say, "I'm sorry". These are the second most powerful words in a successful marriage.
Grandchild:	What are the most powerful words in a marriage?
Grandpa:	"I love you."
Grandchild:	OK, Grandpa, I get the message. Apologies are important in a strong relationship.
Grandpa:	Very perceptive.
Grandchild:	Don't give me too much credit. I will probably still often forget the message. Thanks, Grandpa.

BIG CITY LIFE

Grandchild: Grandpa, did you ever live in a big city?
Grandpa: Only for a short time.
Grandchild: Where was that?
Grandpa: Chicago
Grandchild: Why were you living in Chicago?
Grandpa: I was doing social work at a Boys' Club. We were trying to turn destructive gangs into constructive groups on the near north side of Chicago. It was interesting work.
Grandchild: So, what did you learn about big city life?
Grandpa: I learned three important lessons.
Grandchild: And what were those.
Grandpa: First of all I learned that a big city was really just a lot of small communities jammed together, and each community had its own personality. A neighborhood was often populated by a particular ethnic or racial group, and, of course, there was competition between neighborhoods, just like there is between small towns in the suburbs.
Grandchild: So, what was the difference between competition in small towns and big city neighborhoods?
Grandpa: In the suburbs the competition is usually demonstrated by organized athletic contests, but in big cities the competition often takes place between young gangs in

ASK GRANDPA

	the streets. Our goal at the Boys' Club was to channel this competitive enthusiasm into more organized activities.
Grandchild:	Were you successful?
Grandpa:	Sometimes. I remember one time when we had a basketball tournament at the Club, and a talented group of Italian teens defeated a less talented team of Hungarian Gypsies. The leader of the Gypsies was a boy they called "Greeny", and he announced, after the game, that the gypsies were going to have a rumble with the Italians to establish their superiority, which they hadn't been able to do on the basketball court.
Grandchild:	So what happened?
Grandpa:	I told Greeny that I was going to his house to talk with his parents.
Grandchild:	And did you talk with his parents?
Grandpa:	I did, and I told them that their son was a very talented athlete, but if he continued to use threats when he lost, he wouldn't be a successful athlete. The parents were very receptive, and a very subdued Greeny came home as we were finishing our conversation. There was no rumble.
Grandchild:	So, what happened to Greeny?
Grandpa:	I wish I knew. I didn't remain at the Boys Club very long after that, and when I returned for a reunion years later, nobody seemed to know.
Grandchild:	What else did you learn about the big city?
Grandpa:	I learned a little about big city politics.
Grandchild:	You mean, that they are crooked?
Grandpa:	Probably, but I also learned how a big city is managed.
Grandchild:	And how is it managed?
Grandpa:	By dividing it into smaller units, called precincts, and putting someone in charge of each precinct.
Grandchild:	How does that work?
Grandpa:	It worked very well. One time we needed something for the Boys/ Club and I had to contact the Precinct Committee Chairman, the person who was in charge

of the Precinct in which the Boys Club was located. My request was taken care of right away, and I realized that this was a very efficient way to run a city. Each Precinct Chairman was responsible for keeping his constituents happy, and if he didn't do a good job, he would be replaced.

Grandchild: What was the third thing you learned in the big city?

Grandpa: That, after you have lived in a neighborhood for a while, you are accepted as part of it. I never felt fearful when we lived in Chicago, even though there were some strange characters in our neighborhood, and Gloria would take our small children for walks around the block without encountering any trouble. People are people in big cities as well as in small towns, and most of them are decent folks.

Grandchild: Did you enjoy your time in the city?

Grandpa: I enjoyed the challenge of my job, but I prefer living in a small town.

Grandchild: Why is that?

Grandpa: Because in a small town, it is more likely that you can make a difference and have some influence in what goes on. This is hard to do in a big city.

Grandchild: Anything else you learned in the big city?

Grandpa: I leaned that I was not immune to tuberculosis. Growing up in a small town, I was probably never exposed to it when I was younger. Thus I did not develop any immunity to it when I came in contact with it in the city. It put me in a TB Hospital for 15 months, but that is another story.

Grandchild: Which I will probably hear sometime. Thanks, Grandpa.

CANOEING & RAFTING

Grandchild: Grandpa, after your started your medical practice, did you have any time for family vacations?

Grandpa: We always tried to do something with the family each summer, but the vacations were short and economical. We never had much vacation money, and I couldn't be away from my practice very long because I delivered a lot of babies.

Grandchild: So, what did you do for vacations?

Grandpa: We went canoeing.

Grandchild: With the whole family?

Grandpa: We actually frequently went with two families – my brother Dave's family and ours. Dave and Barb had eight children and there were a lot of matched ages between the two families. Most of the canoes would contain a member of each family and competition was always a big part of our get-togethers. I remember one time when Tony and Brad, both cocky athletic teenagers, decided to demonstrate their superior canoeing ability, so they yelled, "goodbye" and rapidly paddled ahead of the rest of us. They hardly made it past the first turn in the turbulent river before they hit a floating log and tipped over. They were floating in the river with humbled expressions as the rest of us paddled by.

Grandchild: Did you camp out along the river?

Grandpa: We would pitch our camp half way along our route and then return to the starting point to begin canoeing. Our campsite was our destination at the end of the first day. My brother and I were in charge of the food, and our suppers would often be hot dogs or hamburgers cooked over an open fire, supplemented with other tasty morsels, such as baked potatoes or corn on the cob cooked in the hot coals. Of course we would always feast on S'mores before we retired for the night, squashing roasted marshmallows on a chocolate bar between two graham crackers. For breakfast, Dave's specialty was pancakes and mine was French toast. We ate well. Those were fun times.

Grandchild: I think I want to go canoeing. Is it difficult? Do canoes tip easily?

Grandpa: Not usually – unless they are tipped intentionally.

Grandchild: Why would you tip them intentionally?

Grandpa: Splashing people in the other canoes was, of course, common, but sometimes, if one canoe tipped over, the occupants would feel obliged to tip over the other canoes, so their occupants could share the cool refreshing dip in the river.

Grandchild: Did you and grandma ever get tipped over?

Grandpa: We carried the food in our canoe, so tipping us was not allowed.

Grandchild: Very clever.

Grandpa: It's called the privilege of old age.

Grandchild: Did you have any memorable canoeing stories?

Grandpa: Every canoe trip created memories, of course, but I still remember one canoe trip quite vividly. In addition to our large family get-togethers, each summer I would go canoeing for a weekend with just one of our children. These were great bonding experiences because we were on the river without phones, television or radio, and my son or daughter would have to talk to me and listen to

	what I had to say. Since I was in charge of the food, they treated me well..
Grandchild:	So, what was your memorable trip?
Grandpa:	I was canoeing the Two Hearted River in the Michigan's Upper Peninsula with Candi. The river wound through a very remote, densely wooded area on the southern border of Lake Superior. It was beautiful, but wild and desolate, and we didn't see another canoe all day. It was kind of spooky. As we neared the end of the river, a storm came up, the sky darkened, rain began to fall, and the thunder rumbled like an approaching locomotive. We feared we were about to be enveloped in a tornado, so we quickly beached the canoe and clung to the small brush along the side of the river, in hopes of preventing the tornado from twirling us up into the sky. After a while, although the rumble continued, the sky started to clear, the rain stopped and birds were flying without any apparent concern. We decided to climb back into the canoe and try to reach the end of the river safely. We rounded two more turns and arrived at the mouth of the river on the shore of Lake Superior. Our tornado turned out to be the sound of the surf crashing onto the shore. We survived!
Grandchild:	That sounds scary. I heard you also did some whitewater rafting, Did you have any narrow escapes while rafting?
Grandpa:	We had lots of exciting rafting trips on the Youghiogheny (Yough) River in Pennsylvania. Seldom did any of us complete a rafting trip without being dumped in the water. One trip was especially memorable. Your Grandma was in the raft with me, and when we hit the first set of rapids, she flipped out of the raft and hit her hand on a rock on the bottom. I got her back in the raft, advised her the cold river water would soothe the pain and reduce the swelling and then told her to keep paddling – for four more hours! When we returned home, an x-ray disclosed a broken bone in her hand which required surgery to

	insert a metal pin to stabilize the bone. In spite of many apologies from me, she still sometimes reminds me of how insensitive I was to make her keep paddling.
Grandchild:	That _was_ insensitive.
Grandpa:	Now, don't you start in on me. She doesn't need any additional support. There was one other rafting experience that had a funny episode.
Grandchild:	What was that?
Grandpa:	I was in a raft with my son, Tony, and while going through an especially wild rapids, I fell out of the raft. The guide quickly threw me a rope and towed me to shore. I was standing on a rock when another raft went by and one of the occupants yelled, "Look what he did to his feet!" The truth was that I hadn't done anything to my feet. I just have very ugly feet. We all enjoyed a good laugh.
Grandchild:	I think I might enjoy rafting as well as canoeing. Any suggestions?
Grandpa:	If you go canoeing, pick a river that has some active white water rapids. You won't get bored. And if you go rafting, be sure to go on a guided trip first. You will be much safer and better prepared when you go rafting on your own. Each time I rafted with one of my children, we always started with a guided trip first and then did it on our own the next day. And we all survived.
Grandchild:	I have just added two activities to my bucket list. Thanks, Grandpa

CAREERS

Grandchild: Can I ask you a question?
Grandpa: Of course.
Grandchild: What do you think I should do when I grow up?
Grandpa: That's not my decision.
Grandchild: Can't you give me some suggestions?
Grandpa: I could give you a long list of suggestions, but the only one that matters is the one you choose.
Grandchild: When did you decide to become a doctor?
Grandpa: When I was younger than you.
Grandchild: Why did you choose that career?
Grandpa: I had this rather vague idealistic desire to help people, and I thought medicine would give me the opportunity to do that.
Grandchild: I suppose healing people might be the best way to help them.
Grandpa: Actually, it is only one of the ways to help. Most any career you choose has the potential of helping people.
Grandchild: You mean if I decided to run a grocery store, I could help people?
Grandpa: Of course. You would be providing products that people need and also employment for the people you hire to help run the store.
Grandchild: So, you are not going to suggest a career for me?
Grandpa: Nope, because then it would be my choice, not yours.

Grandchild: What if I choose a career and then decide I don't like it?
Grandpa: Then you would be like the majority of people. Most people try at least three different careers before they find the one that works for them.
Grandchild: But you ended up with your first career choice.
Grandpa: Not really. It was my first choice, and that's where I ended up, but that's not where I started. There were a few detours along the way.
Grandchild: Like what?
Grandpa: Well, when I graduated from college, I decided I wasn't smart enough to get into medical school, so I never even applied. Instead, I went to graduate school, earned a Degree in Social Work and ended up working at a Boys Club in Inner City Chicago for three years.
Grandchild: And then you went to medical school?
Grandpa: No, then I taught school for seven years.
Grandchild: You were a teacher?
Grandpa: Yes,
Grandchild: What did you teach?
Grandpa: I taught Science and Math to 7th and 8th Graders.
Grandchild: You tried to teach crazy adolescents? That must have been a challenge.
Grandpa: It was, but I found I really enjoyed it.
Grandchild: So, why did you leave teaching?
Grandpa: I wanted to be a Doctor, remember?
Grandchild: Weren't you too old by then to go to medical school?
Grandpa: I was certainly the oldest person in my medical school class. I was 36 when I started.
Grandchild: That's really old!
Grandpa: You won't think so when you get older.
Grandchild: So why did you suddenly decide you could become a doctor? I thought you didn't think you were smart enough. Did you get smarter as you got older?
Grandpa: Not smarter – just more committed to my goal. You should understand that people don't reach goals simply

	because they are smarter. People reach goals because their goals are important to them, and they are willing to work very hard to achieve them.
Grandchild:	You mean I can't just decide to be something I like, and it will happen?
Grandpa:	Not likely.
Grandchild:	So, how do I decide what to do?
Grandpa:	Your first task is to find a career that you have a passion for.
Grandchild:	Then what?
Grandpa:	Then you must work very hard to achieve it. Success is not an accident. It is mostly hard work,. .
Grandchild:	Maybe I will win the lottery, and then I won't have to worry about any other goals.
Grandpa:	That's not a goal, That's just a dream – and not a very realistic one. Would you feel successful if you won the lottery?
Grandchild:	Oh, Grandpa, you always want to turn things I say into a moral lesson.
Grandpa:	You don't like moral lessons?
Grandchild:	OK, I get it. If I don't work for something, I won't appreciate achieving it.
Grandpa:	Very profound. I think you are growing wiser.
Grandchild:	It's a slow process. And I still don't know what I want to do. Thanks, Grandpa.

CARS

Grandchild: Grandpa, do you like cars?
Grandpa: I like the convenient travel they provide.
Grandchild: If you had your choice of cars, which one would you choose?
Grandpa: The one we have now, but they don't make them anymore.
Grandchild: You mean the Vibe? That's not a very classy car. Why would you choose that one?
Grandpa: Because it's very useful, gets good gas mileage and requires very few repairs.
Grandchild: But you would look more impressive driving a BMW.
Grandpa: My objective in having a car is not to impress people. It's to provide me with reliable and inexpensive transportation. My Vibe is 15 years old and still runs fine. Why would I spend more money to replace the reliable transportation I already have?
Grandchild: You have a point, but I like fancy cars.
Grandpa: I hope you can afford one.
Grandchild: I can't now, but maybe in the future.
Grandpa: Just remember that the purchase price of a car is just the first expense of driving.
Grandchild: What do you mean?
Grandpa: After you purchase a car, the ongoing expenses can be considerable. For starters, car insurance is expensive, and it is more expensive on expensive cars. You will have to

put gas in the car to make it go, and the further you travel, the more that will cost. To keep the car running smoothly, you will need to service it regularly, and that will cost money unless you are handy with cars and can do this yourself. I am not, so servicing my car myself was not an option.

Grandchild: I think I am now getting your wisdom message for today.

Grandpa: Just trying to help you understand the real costs of having the privilege of owning a car.

Grandchild: Did you ever have to do without a car?

Grandpa: For many years after we married we did not have a car. My father gave us his old car when we first got married, but it required repairs we couldn't afford, so we sold it. We had no car during the four years I was in medical school.

Grandchild: How did you get around?

Grandpa: On a bicycle. We lived two miles from the school, and I would ride my bike there several times a day.

Grandchild: How did you do grocery shopping?

Grandpa: The store was only a block from our house, so we borrowed one of the store's shopping carts to bring the groceries home.

Grandchild: Sounds like you had to make some creative adjustments to compensate for not having a car. .

Grandpa: We called it "necessary adaptation". We found we could get along fine without a car. Public transportation often worked fine – especially when we were living in Chicago.

Grandchild: I don't think I could do that.

Grandpa: Do what?

Grandchild: Get along without a car.

Grandpa: You will be amazed at the adjustments you can make when you need to. .

Grandchild: Another bit of wisdom?

Grandpa: Perhaps, but you probably won't understand it until the need arises.

Grandchild: How many cars did you have when you moved to Hillsdale?

Grandpa: We seldom had more than one because that's all we could afford. I could easily walk to the hospital and to my office, and I rode my bike when I had to go someplace else in town. Grandma needed the car more than I did, and, besides, bicycling was good exercise for me. I had baskets on the back of my bike, and I can recall carrying groceries, tools, books and lots of other things in those baskets. My bike sometimes served as a small truck. .

Grandchild: I would rather have a car.

Grandpa: So would I, but we did what we had to do, and we survived. There was one big advantage to having only one car.

Grandchild: And what might that be?

Grandpa: We didn't have to argue with our children about them using the car because that was not an option. I had to have access to the car in case I had to make a house call.

Grandchild: I think what you are telling me is that a car is expensive and it is possible to survive without one.

Grandpa: You <u>were</u> listening.

Grandchild: Of course. I always listen, but, unfortunately, I don't always take your advice. I'm afraid my wisdom is a few years off. Thanks Grandpa.

CHARITY

Grandchild: Are you a charitable person, Grandpa?
Grandpa: What do you mean by charitable?
Grandchild: I mean do give a lot to charity?
Grandpa: Not really.
Grandchild: Then, you must not be very charitable.
Grandpa: So, do you measure charity by the amount of money someone gives to worthy causes?
Grandchild: I guess so.
Grandpa: If someone has a lot of money and gives a lot to charity, do you think they are more charitable than someone who has a little money and gives a little to charity?
Grandchild: I'm not sure I know where you're going with this.
Grandpa: Let's put it this way. Some churches promote a program called tithing. It equates charitable giving to a percentage of your income. Ten percent is a proportion that is frequently encouraged. In this system, no matter how poor or wealthy a person may be, they are encouraged to give ten percent to charity. Obviously, this means that a wealthy person would give much more than a poor person, but they would both be giving the same percentage of their earnings. Do you think that the wealthy person is more charitable?
Grandchild: They both give away the same share of their earnings?
Grandpa: That's right.

Grandchild:	But it would be a greater sacrifice for someone who is poor.
Grandpa:	That's also correct.
Grandchild:	Then, I suppose the poor person would really be more charitable, even though he gave less.
Grandpa:	It sounds like your definition of charity is related more to sacrifice than to amount.
Grandchild:	Not sure how you got me to think that way, but it is an interesting way to look at it.
Grandpa:	I think the bible has a passage along those lines.
Grandchild:	Why did you say you were not very charitable?
Grandpa:	I said I did not give a lot to charity, but I still like to believe that I'm a charitable person. Remember that giving money is only one way to be charitable.
Grandchild:	What are the other ways?
Grandpa:	I think charity is giving something away and expecting nothing in return. This could mean volunteering your time for a worthy cause or using your skill or expertise to help someone out. It might mean forgiving someone or offering a complement. It could mean welcoming a new neighbor with a plate of cookies.
Grandchild:	So, charity doesn't only include giving away money?
Grandpa:	Not at all, and let me give you another pearl of senior wisdom about charity.
Grandchild:	I'm all ears.
Grandpa:	Perfect charity is when you get no reward or recognition for your charitable act.
Grandchild:	What do you mean?
Grandpa:	Many people's generosity is recognized with names on plaques, buildings or on bricks in a walkway; or they may be recognized at special dedication ceremonies. But the anonymous donor is the perfect giver, because his reward will not be received in this life.
Grandchild:	So, he's saving it up for his afterlife.
Grandpa:	You might put it that way.

Grandchild: I just did. Did you ever make an anonymous gift, Grandpa?

Grandpa: If I did and told you, it would no longer be anonymous. However, I can share with you one time we tried to do this because it is no longer a secret. We helped a relative, whose house had burned down, with a gift of some money. We had very little money of our own at that time, so it was quite a sacrifice for us. We told no one and tried our best not to reveal our identity. We sent a money order and even mailed it from another town, so it couldn't be traced. We were thrilled to do this and were very disappointed when, a few years later, the recipients found out who it was. Part of our joy of giving was lessened because of the worldly recognition we received.

Grandchild: So I get more credit if no one knows about my charity.

Grandpa: Maybe not more, but perhaps the credit will come at a different time and place.

Grandchild: Like heavenly credit?

Grandpa: You said it, but, remember, that charity begins at home so be nice to your parents and your siblings.

Grandchild: That's expecting a lot. Thanks, Grandpa.

CHILDREN

Grandchild: Grandpa, why did you and Grandma have so many children?
Grandpa: Because we read "Cheaper by the Dozen" and believed it.
Grandchild: Aw, come on, Grandpa, I'm serious.
Grandpa: Well, so am I. Actually, that was part of it. Your Grandma and I had both read that book and were quite intrigued by it. We agreed that a large family would be a lot of fun.
Grandchild: And was it?
Grandpa: I guess it depends on what you mean by "fun".
Grandchild: Well, are you glad now that you had a large family?
Grandpa: I think your Grandma and I would agree that it has been an interesting journey.
Grandchild: Would you do it again?
Grandpa: We wouldn't want to go through it again, but, yes, we would probably do it again.
Grandchild: Why?
Grandpa: Because it gave us material for our book.
Grandchild: I think you're jesting, but why did you think you could be successful in raising twelve kids?
Grandpa: We were very naïve, as are most parents, since there are no rehearsals for parenting. We thought we would be perfect parents and have perfect children. .
Grandchild: So, how did that work out?
Grandpa: Neither turned out to be true.

Grandchild: And you found out that raising a big family was not quite like it appeared in the book?

Grandpa: Not really. Before we had children of our own, we had all the answers for child-rearing, which we were happy to share with our friends who already had children. But God has a sense of humor, and he decided we needed a little humility, so he sent us children who would make sure we were humbled. We no longer give advice on raising children.

Grandchild: Didn't you learn that before you had all twelve?

Grandpa: That's a good question, but, in reality, we wouldn't give back any of our twelve. They have each contributed much to our lives.

Grandchild: I just can't imagine raising that many children.

Grandpa: Actually, at times we had more than twelve because we had six exchange students from other Countries each spend a year with us while our kids were growing up, and Grandma liked to take in other children from time to time.

Grandchild: Why in the world would you want to take in other children with so many of your own?

Grandpa: Sometimes they were friends of our children who needed a place to stay for a while, and your compassionate Grandma had a hard time turning them away.

Grandchild: I can imagine how some of my aunts or uncles might have been very challenging when they were growing up.

Grandpa: Your observations are correct.

Grandchild: Which ones were the most challenging?

Grandpa: I won't answer that. You'll have to draw your own conclusions.

Grandchild: That's a very diplomatic answer.

Grandpa: Diplomacy is usually a wise response.

Grandchild: How did you and Grandma survive those years?

Grandpa: We enjoyed our children's achievements, and we laughed a lot. We also decided that there are three stages of

	parenting. The first two are challenging and the third one is essential for parental sanity.
Grandchild:	I think you are about to give me your words of wisdom.
Grandpa:	Unfortunately, my wisdom is not transferable. Your parenting knowledge will come from your own experiences with your own children. All I can do is to let you know that there is survival after parenting.
Grandchild:	OK, what are the three stages of parenting?
Grandpa:	The first is when your children are very young, and they are completely dependent on your care. You decide when and what they eat, when they sleep, what clothes they wear and where they go. This is when other people tell you how cute they are, and you enjoy the compliments. The downside of this is that they are completely dependent on your care. You find it is a 24 hour a day responsibility. You need more sleep than you can find time for.
Grandchild:	What is the second stage?
Grandpa:	This is the most difficult stage. It is when your child decides that he or she needs more freedom and wants to make decisions about school, friends and activities. These decisions sometimes are not consistent with what you think is best, and angry disagreements can occur. It is a time of challenge to authority and can cause friction between the two parents, who might not agree on how to handle their challenging child. It is a time when counselors get involved and sometimes reinforce your feelings of inadequacy. In our family, at a time when our teenagers were causing much unrest, your Grandma actually went away for six weeks to stay with her mother. She took the five youngest children with her and left the teenagers behind for me to deal with. She told me that it was either that or she would need psychiatric care. I, of course, approved of her escape to her mother's. It seemed the best of the two options.
Grandchild:	How did that work out?

Grandpa:	Actually, it worked out quite well. Grandma read lots of books about parenting, and the teenagers treated me like a king, since they didn't have their compassionate mom around to intercede. Grandma realized she could not be a friend to her teenaged children. She had to be a mom, and, when she returned, she posted copies of her expectations in every room with agreements from the children on the consequences if their tasks weren't completed. It didn't make the children perfect, but it did clarify her expectations, and she avoided the psychiatrist.
Grandchild:	And what is the third stage of parenting?
Grandpa:	This is when you acknowledge that your children are separate human beings, who will become who they are because of the decisions they make in their own lives. They are not extensions of you, and you will no longer take the blame for what they do. You admit to yourself that you may not have been a perfect parent but reassure yourself that you did the best you could. You did not do anything to intentionally cause harm to your children. It is only when you reach this stage that you can relax a little and not blame yourself or your spouse for the dumb things your children do.
Grandchild:	I don't think I want to have twelve children.
Grandpa:	Probably a wise decision.
Grandchild:	Thanks, Grandpa.

CHOICES

Grandchild: Grandpa, what determines what kind of a person I am?
Grandpa: Your choices
Grandchild: What about my circumstances. Doesn't that play a part in who I am.
Grandpa: No. Your choices define your character. Circumstances simply reveal it.
Grandchild: So, I can't blame my circumstances for what kind of a person I am?
Grandpa: Let me ask you a question. Are you totally trapped in your circumstances?
Grandchild: What do you mean?
Grandpa: Do you think you have any control over your circumstances? In other words, can you change where you live, where you work, how you spend your money or who you associate with?
Grandchild: I guess so.
Grandpa: Then, really, you are in charge of what kind of a person you are. People, throughout time, have overcome difficult circumstances to become great people. They didn't let their obstacles define them. You have the same opportunity.
Grandchild: So, it's up to me.
Grandpa: I think you get the message.
Grandchild: I'm not sure that I always like your messages.

Grandpa:	Why not?
Grandchild:	Because you always make me feel responsible for who I become.
Grandpa:	What a novel concept.
Grandchild:	OK, so how do I become a better person?
Grandpa:	By making good choices.
Grandchild:	How do I know which are the good choices?
Grandpa:	Most of the time you will know the right choice. You have a built in mechanism for determining right and wrong. It's called, "my conscience". It's like a road sign that appears frequently along your journey through life. You can ignore it, but it is still there in spite of your reluctance to observe it.
Grandchild:	Can I claim ignorance?
Grandpa:	You can claim it, but you know you don't really believe it.
Grandchild:	Why not? The rightness or wrongness of some of my decisions is not very clear.
Grandpa:	So, how do you decide?
Grandchild:	By the results of the decision, I guess. If the results are good, I assume it was a good decision.
Grandpa:	That is called, "Wisdom" which you will acquire when you get older and will have had the opportunity to make many of those decisions.
Grandchild:	Have you ever made a bad decision.
Grandpa:	Haven't we all. One time I spent $4,000 for a travel plan we never used.
Grandchild:	Have you made some good decisions?
Grandpa:	My best decision was to marry your Grandma.
Grandchild:	I will agree with that. I guess your message today is that it's up to me to make the good choices that will make me a better person. Sounds like a lot of personal responsibility, but I will try. Thanks, Grandpa.

COMMUNES

Grandchild: Grandpa, what's a Commune?
Grandpa: Why do you ask?
Grandchild: Somebody told me that is was the perfect way to live.
Grandpa: Did they say why it was the perfect way to live?
Grandchild: He told me that in a Commune everyone is equal and happy.
Grandpa: Sounds like Utopia.
Grandchild: What's Utopia?
Grandpa: It was a word invented centuries ago to represent a perfect living environment.
Grandchild: Sounds like a good goal.
Grandpa: You are not the first one who has said that. Through the years, many people have attempted to create the perfect living environment through governments or by forming small communities of people who seek the same goal. Governmental approaches usually embrace a form of Socialism and small groups are referred to as Communes.
Grandchild: So, what do people do to make a Utopia?
Grandpa: They try to eliminate differences.
Grandchild: What do you mean by that?
Grandpa: Well, the government or the individuals in small groups establish a system where everybody shares equally in everything.
Grandchild: Sounds like a good goal.

Grandpa: The problem is that it doesn't work.
Grandchild: Why not?
Grandpa: In order to give something away, you have to have something to give away. In a nation or in a small commune, where would this "something" come from?
Grandchild: I guess it would come from the people in the group.
Grandpa: That's right. Do you think everyone would contribute the same amount?
Grandchild: Probably not because some people would have more to contribute.
Grandpa: In most communes, when people join, they contribute everything they have to the Commune. This includes not only their money but also their furniture, their clothing, their car and all other possessions. They no longer would have personal ownership of anything. It all belongs to the Community.
Grandchild: Why would they do that?
Grandpa: Because the Commune would then provide for all their needs, like food and lodging.
Grandchild: I don't think I would want to share my toothbrush.
Grandpa: You could probably keep your toothbrush. No one else would want it.
Grandchild: How would the Commune support itself?
Grandpa: They would have to develop ways to make money.
Grandchild: Who would do the work?
Grandpa: The members of the Commune.
Grandchild: Suppose someone refused to work but still wanted to receive the benefits?
Grandpa: You have just described one of the problems with this system of living. Not everyone has the same work ethic. Because of this, a Commune, in order to survive, usually has to establish a work credit system, so that everyone has to contribute an equal share of work.
Grandchild: What if they refuse?

Grandpa:	They may be asked to leave the Commune or could be denied some of the benefits.
Grandchild:	So, if you don't work, you don't eat? Kind of like those of us who don't live in a Commune.
Grandpa:	That's true.
Grandchild:	Why would anyone want to live in a Commune?
Grandpa:	I suppose they have different reasons. They might want to live with a smaller group of people who have more common interests, or they may just want more freedom from the busy competitive life in which most of us live.
Grandchild:	They don't like competition?
Grandpa:	In communal living everyone is considered equal, so competition is not encouraged. In one commune, volleyball was a popular activity, but they didn't keep score. They didn't want to have winners and losers.
Grandchild:	That wouldn't work for me. I like competition.
Grandpa:	I think most people do. Not only in sports but also in life. Most of us want to be rewarded for our own efforts. In a Commune, that wouldn't be encouraged. Everything you did would be for the benefit of the Community.
Grandchild:	So, do people living in a Commune have more freedom?
Grandpa:	Probably not. The Commune requires rules and restrictions in order to make the system work because people have different motivations. Therefore, there has to be a system to resolve these differences. They may avoid government controls, but they still require controls. In a way, these challenges may be more difficult because they have to resolve them with people with whom they are living.
Grandchild:	Did you ever want to live in a Commune, Grandpa?
Grandpa:	Not as described here, but we all live in communities – our families, our towns, our States and our Nation. These are all really communities which require organization and rules but also provide a lot of freedom to choose your own path in life. I'll stay where I am.
Grandchild:	So will I. Thanks, Grandpa.

DEATH PENALTY

Grandchild: Grandpa, do you favor the death penalty?

Grandpa: You mean putting people to death because of some crime they have committed?

Grandchild: Yeah. Since you are pro-life, I wondered how you felt about that.

Grandpa: I've actually changed my mind on that issue.

Grandchild: What made you change your mind?

Grandpa: Well, for most of my life I thought it was appropriate to put some people to death for the terrible crimes they had committed. Why should they live while their victims died?

Grandchild: That's how I feel. So how do you feel now?

Grandpa: Two things have made me oppose the death penalty.

Grandchild: What were those?

Grandpa: First of all, my son, Tony, challenged me. He asked me how I could be pro-life and still favor the death penalty.

Grandchild: What did you tell him?

Grandpa: I told him that an unborn child was innocent, but a criminal was guilty, so they were different issues. However, his question did trouble me and made me think again about my support of executing the guilty.

Grandchild: What else made you change?

Grandpa: I read a book.

Grandchild: What book?

Grandpa: The title was "Dead Man Walking". It was actually made into a movie.

Grandchild: What was the book about?

Grandpa: It was a documentary, written by Sister PreJean, a Nun who followed two different men on death row in a Florida prison. Both had committed heinous crimes and certainly deserved the maximum punishment, and both were executed. Sister PreJean visited each of them a number of times in an attempt to get to know them and, perhaps, to understand why they had committed their crimes. One of them regretted what he had done; the other never did. She also did a lot of research to determine what the justification was for the death penalty.

Grandchild: And what did she decide was the justification?

Grandpa: I'll ask you the question she asked herself. What do you think is the justification for executing a criminal?

Grandchild: It guarantees that he will not commit any more crimes. People will be safer.

Grandpa: That's true, but wouldn't life in prison do the same thing?

Grandchild: Sure, but why should we spend tax money housing and feeding them for rest or their lives? It seems like we could save a lot of money if we executed them.

Grandpa: Statistics actually show that it costs a lot more to execute someone than it does to house and feed them.

Grandchild: Why?

Grandpa: Because of all the expensive legal challenges, and prisoners often spend many years on death row before they are finally executed. Some even die before their execution date.

Grandchild: OK, so it costs more, but wouldn't people be discouraged from committing crimes if they knew they could be executed.

Grandpa: Not true. Studies have shown that the death penalty seems to offer little deterrence to the commission of crimes. Since some States have the death penalty and

	some don't, we can make comparisons, and States that have the death penalty, have just as many serious crimes as the States that don't.
Grandchild:	So, the death penalty doesn't save money, and it doesn't discourage crime.
Grandpa:	That's right, and there is one other concern about the death penalty.
Grandchild:	What's that?
Grandpa:	Sometimes a person who is sentenced to death is not guilty, but this may not be discovered until years later. In these cases, an innocent person could be put to death.
Grandchild:	So what did Sister PreJean conclude was the main justification for the death penalty?
Grandpa:	Revenge! She concluded that the main reason for executions was to "get even' with the criminal by taking his life.
Grandchild:	So, the proper punishment for a murderer is to kill him?
Grandpa:	That's what she concluded, and it made me re-think my own feelings about the death penalty. I finally decided that, since we can remove criminals from society by putting them in prison, I can't condone killing a human being even if that human being was convicted of a terrible crime.
Grandchild:	Not sure that I agree, but you have provided me with a different perspective.
Grandpa:	That was my purpose.
Grandchild:	Thanks, Grandpa.

FAITH

Grandchild: Grandpa, do you really believe there is a God.
Grandpa: Don't you?
Grandchild: Well, I have trouble believing in something I can't see or prove.
Grandpa: Do you believe your mother loves you?
Grandchild: Of course.
Grandpa: Why do you believe that?
Grandchild: Because she's my mother.
Grandpa: What is your proof that she loves you?
Grandchild: She does a lot of nice things to take care of me.
Grandpa: Maybe God does nice things for you, too.
Grandchild: But I can't see God. I can see mom.
Grandpa: Do you think your mom ever does nice things for you when you can't see her?
Grandchild: Of course. I didn't see her fix my lunch, but it was on the table when I left for school.
Grandpa: Maybe God does the same thing.
Grandchild: You mean fix my lunch?
Grandpa: I don't think God makes sandwiches. But he may protect you when you do something foolish.
Grandchild: Like riding my bike too fast down the hill and nearly running into a tree?
Grandpa: You didn't get hurt, did you? Perhaps God protected you.
Grandchild: You can't prove that.

Grandpa:	Nor can you prove that he didn't.
Grandchild:	Grandpa, you always twist whatever I say into something else.
Grandpa:	I just try to share with you another way to look at the situation.
Grandchild:	So, why do you believe in a God you can't see?.
Grandpa:	It's called Faith.
Grandchild:	What is Faith?
Grandpa:	It's believing in something you can't prove. Like you, I would like to be able to prove that God exists. I've spent more years than you trying to do that without success. I'm not alone. Many people have tried to prove the existence of God.
Grandchild:	So why do you believe in God?
Grandpa:	Well, I have two choices. Either God exists and has an impact on my life or he doesn't and everything is up to me. Since often I need help, I choose to hope that God is there.
Grandchild:	That's a rather simplistic view of God – as helper.
Grandpa:	Sometimes simple is the best way to look at things.
Grandchild:	What if there really is no God?
Grandpa:	I don't lose anything by believing in God, and he left a pretty good guide for a happy life.
Grandchild:	You mean the Ten Commandments?
Grandpa:	Yes. You do believe they are a good guide for life, don't you?
Grandchild:	Yes, I suppose so. Do you believe there is really a Heaven?
Grandpa:	Why shouldn't I.
Grandchild:	Because you can't prove it exists.
Grandpa:	You're still hung up on proving things, aren't you?
Grandchild:	Of course.
Grandpa:	Well, I look at it this way. If there is no Heaven, but I follow the Ten Commandments, what have I lost? If there is a Heaven and I choose not to follow the Ten Commandments, then what have I lost?.
Grandchild:	I hate your logical answers.
Grandpa:	Why?
Grandchild:	Because they're logical. Thanks, Grandpa.

FAMILY VACATIONS

Grandchild: Grandpa, did you ever take vacations with your kids?

Grandpa: Sure did, and I always promised them that they would have a unique experience. Sometimes it would be a good experience and sometimes it would be a challenging experience but, whichever it was, it would never be duplicated.

Grandchild: How did you travel with twelve kids?

Grandpa: Well, we never really travelled with all twelve. When I was in Medical School, one summer we took a trip to Colorado with nine of them. The youngest three weren't born yet.

Grandchild: You must have had a big motor home.

Grandpa: That would certainly have made the trip much easier. We actually travelled west in a used Ford Station Wagon and a rented fold-down camper.

Grandchild: Where did you put everybody?

Grandpa: The Station Wagon had three seats, so three people sat in each seat and the youngest two rode in the luggage area behind the rear seat. Unfortunately, we didn't have window seats for everyone, so there was always controversy over the seating arrangement..

Grandchild: Where did you put your luggage?

Grandpa: We had a luggage carrier on the roof of the Station Wagon for whatever we couldn't fit into the trailer.

Grandchild: Did you stop at motels at night?

Grandpa: Oh no, we had $120 for the twelve days of the trip, so we stayed in $1.50/night campgrounds and enjoyed free public playgrounds and parks, whenever possible. We prepared our meals over a Coleman stove, while the kids explored the campground and met our new temporary neighbors.

Grandchild: Where did everybody sleep?

Grandpa: Our sleeping arrangements were challenging. After our evening meal, we would prepare wall to wall beds in the camper, and the two older boys would sleep in the back of the Station Wagon. If you were sleeping in the trailer and had to go to the bathroom in the middle of the night, you had to climb over the other slumbering bodies to get out. Unfortunately, some of the younger children didn't make the effort; so wet beds were a much too frequent occurrence. It was not a pleasant feeling to feel the moisture creep over to your side of the bed, and changing wet clothes and remaking the bed in the dark was a monumental task.

Grandchild: You took this vacation trip on purpose?

Grandpa: We did, but I had enjoyed vacation trips with my mother when I was growing up. She was very organized and made the journeys seem easy. Of course, on those trips we travelled with only four. I naively thought that camping with my family, even though three times as large, would be equally simple. I was wrong. One night was particularly memorable, but the humor of the episode was not appreciated until much later. We had traveled farther than usual that day in an effort to reach Pike's Peak, so when we pulled into a campsite part way up the mountain, it was already dark. We were all tired, hungry and irritable, and, to make things worse, we couldn't find our flashlight, and our lantern didn't work. During the night, two of the kids each wet their beds twice, two others were sick to their stomachs, and some animal made off with all of our meat from the cooler which we had placed outside. Nobody got much sleep that night, and our grocery stash was greatly depleted. Fortunately, a College classmate of mine came to the rescue. He lived a short distance away, so we visited him, his wife and their eight children. They fed us hamburgers and steaks, our kids had great fun playing with their new young friends and we went back to our trailer with a flashlight and a lantern that worked.

Grandchild: Why in the world did you take that trip anyway?

Grandpa: I was told that family vacations bring families closer together, and this trip certainly accomplished that. However, I was thinking of emotional closeness, not physical closeness. The trip kept us in very close proximity for 12 days. On the last day, we drove over 600 miles to reach home, so we wouldn't have to spend another night in the camper!

Grandchild: So, you never took another vacation trip?

Grandpa: I guess we were slow learners because a week after we returned from our trip west, we took the family for a long weekend to visit some of Grandma's relatives in Arkansas. However, this time we stayed in a large housekeeping cabin at a State Park. It was a much more peaceful experience, and we decided that staying in one place is much more pleasant than travelling every day..

Grandchild: Other than the trauma of travelling with nine children, did you have any memorable experiences?

Grandpa: We had one unusual experience during the trip to Arkansas which, I suspect, still creates nightmares for some of the children. One evening, at dusk, while I was driving, I noticed hundreds of small creatures crawling across the road. I suddenly realized they were tarantula spiders! I awakened my slumbering family to view this spectacle and received drowsy comments questioning the credibility of my observations. Finally, I stopped the car and suggested they open the car door and look more closely. The door remained open only briefly, and there were terrified screams as my observation was confirmed. The whole family was quickly wide-awake, and there were frantic appeals for me to keep the car moving before the spiders found their way in. Apparently we had encountered a rare migration of tarantulas that even most of the locals had never seen.

Grandchild: I'm glad I wasn't along on that trip. I don't like spiders. OK, Grandpa, what are your words of wisdom from your family camping trips?

Grandpa: I'm sure there must be a few pearls, but all I can come up with are these two:
Don't expect to have the same experience travelling with eleven that you did growing up, travelling with four.
Pitch camp and stay in one place or stay home and enjoy the local lake.

Grandchild: Were there any benefits?

Grandpa: Of course. Had we not gone on those trips, our kids would not have those unforgettable memories, and I wouldn't have material for this blog.

Grandchild: Thanks, Grandpa.

FAVORITE CHILD

Grandchild: Grandpa, which of your children is your favorite?
Grandpa: I won't answer that.
Grandchild: Why not?
Grandpa: If I named one, I would have eleven people angry with me.
Grandchild: But, surely, you must have your favorites.
Grandpa: Let me put it this way. I like to think that I love my children equally, but I don't necessarily like their behaviors equally.
Grandchild: Not sure I understand the difference.
Grandpa: The love of a parent for his or her child is special and is present at birth. It is a bond that never goes away and continues regardless of the child's behavior. It is more enduring than any other human relationship, but it is somewhat different for a father and a mother. A mother's love is unique because the mother nourished and provided a home for the child before the child was born, while a father's love is more often influenced by the behavior of the child after birth.
Grandchild: So, my mother loves me more than my father.
Grandpa: Not more – just differently.
Grandchild: It sounds like mothers love unconditionally, but a father's love is dependent on the child's behavior.
Grandpa: I hadn't really thought of it that way, but I think you're right.

Grandchild: Hey, maybe I am sharing some of my wisdom with you.
Grandpa: Don't be overly impressed. Everyone displays wisdom sometimes.
Grandchild: OK, let's get back to your kids. You love them equally, but you don't accept their behavior equally.
Grandpa: That's correct. Sometimes we have to tell our children that we love them, but we don't like them.
Grandchild: It sounds like if I want my father to like me, I better behave myself, but my mother will like me no matter what I do.
Grandpa: Perhaps you're not as wise as you thought. Your mother's love may be unconditional, but her liking you will still depend on your behavior. She may have a softer shoulder (and paddle) than dad, but her feelings for you are still influenced by what you do.
Grandchild: So, Grandpa, can you tell me which of your children you like the best?
Grandpa: Nope
Grandchild: You're afraid I will tell the other kids, aren't you?
Grandpa: I guess that's part of my wisdom. Besides, thru the years, different children have provided us with reasons to applaud them, so if I chose one now, it would only be temporary.
Grandchild: OK, I get the message – you are not going to answer my question.
Grandpa: Very perceptive of you.
Grandchild: Thanks anyway, Grandpa.

FREE ENTERPRISE

Grandchild: Grandpa, what is free enterprise?
Grandpa: Why are you asking?
Grandchild: One of my friends said it is the freedom for merchants to rip off their customers.
Grandpa: And how did your friend say this was going to be accomplished?
Grandchild: He said that merchants could overcharge for their products because there was no limit on how much they could charge.
Grandpa: What did your friend say was the solution for this over-charging?
Grandchild: He thought the government should limit how much could be charged.
Grandpa: That's called price control, and it's been tried more than once.
Grandchild: Did it work?
Grandpa: Not very well, and the merchants certainly didn't like it.
Grandchild: Why not?
Grandpa: They thought that competition was a fairer way of controlling prices.
Grandchild: How did it do that?
Grandpa: Well, let's say that you found a good way to produce a product that somebody else was also producing. How would you determine how much to sell it for?

ASK GRANDPA

Grandchild: I suppose I would want to sell it for enough that I could make a decent profit.

Grandpa: Your competitor has the same objective. And how do you think customers will decide whose product to buy?

Grandchild: If the products were the same quality, they would probably buy the cheapest one.

Grandpa: That is what we call free enterprise or a market economy. Customers and competition then keep prices under control

Grandchild: Suppose I am the only one producing a product.

Grandpa: In that case, you can charge whatever you want, but there are still limits. People may want your product, but they can't afford it or they simply choose not to buy it at the price you are charging. Since a business needs customers in order to succeed, you then may have to reduce the price so more people will purchase it. As long as you are not forced to sell at a certain price, this is also free enterprise.

Grandchild: What don't you like about the Government setting the price?

Grandpa: What would the government know about your business?

Grandchild: I suppose the government might compare it with similar businesses and decide what a fair price is.

Grandpa: That's what customers do, and they do a better job than the government. They decide if a product is overpriced. If it is, they don't buy it. If enough people don't buy it, the merchant will get the message loud and clear if he wants to stay in business, and he will lower the price.

Grandchild: My friend didn't explain it that way.

Grandpa: That's because your young friend has never had his own business.

Grandchild: You're right. I guess free enterprise works pretty well. Thanks Grandpa.

GAMBLING

Grandchild: Grandpa, did you ever gamble?
Grandpa: I was a big gambler. I fathered 12 children!
Grandchild: That's not gambling.
Grandpa: It sure is. Raising children is probably the biggest gamble you can take.
Grandchild: Aw, come on Grandpa; you know what I mean. Did you gamble with money?
Grandpa: I bet on a horse race once.
Grandchild: Why just once?
Grandpa: Because the horse won, and I didn't want to lose my winnings.
Grandchild: But you didn't have the fun of trying to pick winning horses in the other races.
Grandpa: Oh, yes I did. I picked horses in every other race, but I didn't bet any money on them, and they all lost. Because I didn't spend any money on those losers and never again bet on a horse race, I am still a winner at the racetrack.
Grandchild: Didn't you ever dream of winning the lottery?
Grandpa: Sure, but I never will.
Grandchild: Why not?
Grandpa: Because I never buy a ticket.
Grandchild: Why don't you buy a ticket? Don't you want to have a chance to win the big money?

Grandpa:	Sure, but I would like better odds than a million to one. If I make a bet with you, I have a 50-50 chance of winning. I like those odds better.
Grandchild:	Your payoff would be pretty small if you bet with me.
Grandpa:	That's true, but I would have the satisfaction of winning more often.
Grandchild:	Sometimes your logic amuses me.
Grandpa:	Why do you think people gamble?
Grandchild:	I guess it's because they dream of a big payday.
Grandpa:	Correct. It's human nature to want to get something for nothing. Gambling is the legal way to become rich overnight.
Grandchild:	I guess that's why lotteries are so popular.
Grandpa:	That's right, but I have a problem with the government encouraging people to gamble.
Grandchild:	But the earnings go for education. Isn't that a good cause?
Grandpa:	I find that an interesting rationalization. That means we don't have to be concerned about what we do as long as there is some benefit attached to it.
Grandchild:	I think you are trying to lead me into one of your logic traps.
Grandpa:	Just trying to understand where you are coming from. You are using the age old argument that the end justifies the means.
Grandchild:	What do you mean by that?
Grandpa:	Well, if we can find some benefit from an activity, we don't have to judge whether the activity itself is good or bad.
Grandchild:	So, if gambling is wrong, then the fact that it has the benefit of supporting education doesn't make it right.
Grandpa:	I think you are getting the message.
Grandchild:	Why is gambling wrong?
Grandpa:	The trouble is not that gambling itself is wrong. It can be an enjoyable form of entertainment. It's just that many of the people who gamble can't afford to lose money, and

they get addicted into thinking that they are going to win big with the next roll of the dice. While their losses produce the profits that support education, these losses also produce financial hardships for their families. I don't think the proper role of government is to encourage destructive behavior.

Grandchild: I never thought of it that way. Maybe you have a point. Do you approve of gambling at all?

Grandpa: If you can afford it.

Grandchild: What do you mean?

Grandpa: For some people, gambling is a form of recreation, and they spend money on a card game, a roll of the dice or a spin of the roulette wheel to try to win more money. They enjoy winning, but they treat it as a game and not as a way to earn a living. They consider it a form of entertainment – like going to a movie or a play or a ballgame – or bowling or playing golf. They limit the amount of money they spend, and when that is gone, they go home. Unfortunately, there are others who gamble beyond their means and end up spending money they can't afford to lose while seeking an unlikely pot of gold. If you can't afford to lose any money, you shouldn't be gambling.

Grandchild: So, treating gambling as entertainment is ok, but pursuing it to become a millionaire is not?

Grandpa: I think you have just found your pearl of wisdom for today.

Grandchild: Thanks, Grandpa.

GENEROSITY

Grandchild: Grandpa, are you a generous person?
Grandpa: It depends on what you mean by "generous".
Grandchild: Well, do you donate a lot of time and money?
Grandpa: I suppose I'm about average in that regard. Many people are more generous than I, and many people are less generous. Speaking of generosity, do you realize what a generous Country you live in?
Grandchild: What do you mean?
Grandpa: People in the United States are probably more generous than people in any other Nation.
Grandchild: But aren't we one of the richest Nations? We should be more generous.
Grandpa: That's true, but there is another reason.
Grandchild: What's that?
Grandpa: We don't expect the Government to do everything for us, so when other people have needs, we feel an obligation to help with our donation of time and money.
Grandchild: What about our Welfare system? That's a Government program to help people in need.
Grandpa: That's true, and it has certainly had an impact on our need to be generous.
Grandchild: What do you mean?
Grandpa: Let me give you an example in my medical practice. When I first started my practice, we didn't have

	Medicaid. That's the Government program that provides free medical care to poor people.
Grandchild:	You mean poor people get free medical care?
Grandpa:	They do now. But that wasn't true when I first started. If a poor mother brought two of her sick children in for me to take care of, I would often see both but charge her for only one, or I might not charge her at all. .
Grandchild:	That was quite generous of you.
Grandpa:	I was not unique. Most doctors at that time would do the same because we knew a poor patient would have trouble paying the full charge. But then Medicaid arrived, and my attitude changed.
Grandchild:	In what way?
Grandpa:	Now I knew the patient was not paying the bill – the Government was, and I had little incentive to save the Government money. So I charged the full amount, knowing that the Government payment would be less than what I charged. I no longer felt a need to be generous.
Grandchild:	So, if the Government takes care of the needy, there is less desire or need to be generous.
Grandpa:	I think you are actually showing some understanding of the motivation for generosity.
Grandchild:	Don't give me too much credit. I'm still in the learning phase. Let me see if I understand. If the Government will take care of other people's needs, we don't need to worry about helping them ourselves.
Grandpa:	Your understanding amazes me. That is the downside of Socialism. If all of people's needs are taken care of by the Government, our incentive for generosity is greatly reduced.
Grandchild:	And, if being generous is a good quality, our opportunity to be good is reduced if the Government provides for the poor.
Grandpa:	Your analysis is impressive.

Grandchild:	Don't be so impressed because you led me into that analysis. I didn't do it on my own.
Grandpa:	At least that means you were listening.
Grandchild:	That's because I started this conversation. Okay, do I understand that you are against welfare programs?
Grandpa:	Not completely. I am not against the government using my tax money to help people who really need the help because of mental or physical disabilities. However, I am against welfare for people, who don't have these disabilities and yet are living on government welfare with little incentive to do otherwise. Star Parker, an intelligent African American, who accepted welfare for a few years when she was young, finally realized that she had become enslaved by the welfare system. She stopped her welfare existence and later wrote a book titled "Uncle Sam's Cabin" that suggested that Government welfare was the worst thing that has happened to the African American community because it took away people's incentive to work and enslaved them.
Grandchild:	Wow, I didn't expect to get a lecture on welfare.
Grandpa:	Just remember, that human nature being what it is, some people will seek the easy way. Welfare can be a tempting route, but it often arrives at a dead end.
Grandchild:	So, you think welfare is alright for people who need it but not for freeloaders?
Grandpa:	I think you have defined my opinion very accurately.
Grandchild:	Just a lucky guess. Thanks, Grandpa.

GOODNESS

Grandchild: Grandpa, am I a good person?
Grandpa: I can't answer that.
Grandchild: You don't think I'm a good person?
Grandpa: That's not your question.
Grandchild: What do you mean?
Grandpa: You asked if you were a good person. Only you can answer that. When you ask, "Do you think I'm a good person" you are asking for my opinion.
Grandchild: What's the difference?
Grandpa: What other people think of you is your reputation. What you know about yourself is your character. No one knows who you really are better than you. You can fool other people, but you can't really fool yourself. So only you know if you are good.
Grandchild: How do I know if I am good?
Grandpa: It all depends on what you consider good. What would be your criteria for being good?
Grandchild: I guess being nice to other people would be good.
Grandpa: That's a good start. What else?
Grandchild: Being obedient to my parents.
Grandpa: Your parents would certainly appreciate that.
Grandchild: Working hard at a job would probably be a good thing.
Grandpa: Your employer would appreciate that.

Grandchild:	Not losing my temper would be a nice goal, but I might not be very good at that.
Grandpa:	But you can work on that one. I think it is safe to say that not one of us is perfectly good. We all have things we can work on to become better.
Grandchild:	Good! That means there's hope for me.
Grandpa:	And for all of us. There was only one perfect man in history, and he was nailed to a cross.
Grandchild:	Ouch! Maybe I don't want to be perfect.
Grandpa:	Do you think the Ten Commandments are a pretty good guide for goodness?
Grandchild:	Sure, but most of them tell me what not to do, rather than what I should do.
Grandpa:	Let me give you the positive message from the Ten Commandments in just three words.
Grandchild:	In just three words? What might those be?
Grandpa:	JUST BE NICE.
Grandchild:	You mean that's your abbreviation for the Ten Commandments?
Grandpa:	It turns the "Do nots" into "dos", doesn't it?
Grandchild:	I guess so.
Grandpa:	The only thing it doesn't cover is the part about honoring God, but that is also a positive message.
Grandchild:	Grandpa, sometimes I wonder how you come up with these logical explanations.
Grandpa:	Because I have lived a long life.
Grandchild:	Will I be smarter when I get older?
Grandpa:	Maybe not smarter but, hopefully, wiser. Let me ask you a question.
Grandchild:	I thought I was asking the questions.
Grandpa:	Now it's my turn.
Grandchild:	Ok, what do you want to ask me?
Grandpa:	What do you think is the most important characteristic you can have for both your goodness and your reputation?

Grandchild: I can think of a lot of things, but they probably won't be right, so tell me what is most important.
Grandpa: Integrity.
Grandchild: What does that mean?
Grandpa: It means that people can always trust you.
Grandchild: You mean I should always be truthful, even if it causes me pain or disappointment?
Grandpa: I think you are getting the message.
Grandchild: Why is that so important?
Grandpa: Because if people can trust you, they will always respect you, even if they may not agree with you about everything. On the other hand, if you do something that causes them to distrust you, they will probably always distrust you. This applies to marriage, work, school and all relationships you will have during your life.
Grandchild: You mean my integrity, or lack of it, will stay with me for a long time. I think I understand. I will try hard to protect mine. Thanks, Grandpa.

IMMIGRATION

Grandchild: Grandpa, how do you feel about the immigration controversy going on today?

Grandpa: That's a big question, without simple answers. Unfortunately, it has become very emotional and political, and it is difficult to engage in a rational discussion because people have become so polarized.

Grandchild: That's why I am asking for your opinion because you are usually pretty rational.

Grandpa: Thanks, but the first requirement of a rational discussion is that accurate information has to be available on which to base the discussion.

Grandchild: And where do we get this accurate information?

Grandpa: Good question. If we have strong feelings about a topic, we usually get our information from sources that agree with us and it is difficult to find totally unbiased sources – if we even want to find them.

Grandchild: So, how about immigration?

Grandpa: If you listen to some sources, we are unfairly preventing Muslims from entering our Country, tearing children away from their parents and confining people in Nazi-like concentration camps. If you listen to others, we are protecting our Country by preventing criminals from entering, we are confining, in a humane way, people who enter the Country illegally and we are evaluating them

	to see if they can remain or should be sent back to their Countries of origin.
Grandchild:	So, how do we know who to believe?
Grandpa:	You are full of good questions today.
Grandchild:	That's because I'm confused.
Grandpa:	Join the crowd. Confusion is common on this issue. To have a meaningful discussion about a topic, you need to find a starting point on which you can agree and then be willing to listen to other people's opinions. Most issues are not black and white, so there is probably some truth on both sides of any argument. .
Grandchild:	So, how do we use this logic on immigration?
Grandpa:	Let's approach this issue on a more personal level. First of all, can we agree that we have the right to limit who comes into our homes?
Grandchild:	Of course. That's why many people lock their doors. I wouldn't want just anyone walking into my house.
Grandpa:	Would you want to exclude criminals?
Grandchild:	Certainly.
Grandpa:	What about a hungry small child who knocks on your door and asks for food?
Grandchild:	OK, now you are trying to reach my emotions and challenge my compassionate nature. I would have trouble turning the child away.
Grandpa:	Suppose the child's parents were with her. Would you let them come in with her?
Grandchild:	I don't know about that. I know nothing about them. They might not be honest people and are just using their child to get me to let them in my house. I might let the child in but not the parents.
Grandpa:	So, you would separate the child from her parents!
Grandchild:	Only temporarily until I can decide whether my family is safe with the parents in my home.
Grandpa:	How would you determine that?

Grandchild: I might talk to them – or to my neighbors – or contact the local police department to find out more about them.

Grandpa: Isn't that what we do with illegal immigrants at our border?

Grandchild: I guess so.

Grandpa: The immigration dilemma is really about compassion versus safety. Our compassionate nature encourages us to help people, but we also want to feel that our family is safe. Unfortunately, many people today only want to focus on one side of the issue – either the compassion or the safety, and that produces some intense and angry interactions. Often it is politically motivated.

Grandchild: Why can't we be both compassionate and safe?

Grandpa: Good question.

Grandchild: Can't we agree on some things, and then compromise on things we don't agree on?

Grandpa: You are sounding like a politician.

Grandchild: I think we could all agree that we don't want to let known criminals come into our Country, but we could also probably agree that we don't want to exclude good people who are looking for better lives.

Grandpa: I think you have framed the controversy very well.

Grandchild: You mean I have actually displayed some wisdom?

Grandpa: Yes, and I think I will vote for you.

Grandchild: Thanks, Grandpa, but I'm not running for office..

IMPORTANT PEOPLE

Grandchild: Grandpa, how do you want people to remember you?

Grandpa: Wow, that's a rather profound question from a young person. Actually, I have asked some of my contemporaries that same question, and I have received a variety of answers. One person wanted to be remembered for being a good teacher, someone else wanted to be remembered as being compassionate and a third person wanted to be remembered as always being honest and fair to other people.

Grandchild: So, what about you?

Grandpa: I thought long and hard about this before I came up with my answer.

Grandchild: And what was that?

Grandpa: I decided that I wanted to be remembered as someone who made a difference.

Grandchild: What do you mean by "made a difference?"

Grandpa: Well, I guess I was hoping that my presence in this world was important in some way.

Grandchild: You mean, will you be missed? I can assure you that you will be missed, Grandpa.

Grandpa: Thanks. I appreciate that.

Grandchild: Did anyone make a difference in your life?

Grandpa: You are full of profound questions today.

Grandchild: Not sure I'm capable of being profound but thanks for the compliment.

Grandpa: I sometimes ask people who made a difference in their lives, and there is one profession that seems to be mentioned most often.

Grandchild: And what is that?

Grandpa: Teachers. Almost everyone will name at least one teacher or coach who has had a significant impact on his or her life. They don't usually mention their doctor.

Grandchild: Why do you think that is so?

Grandpa: I suppose it is because few people, other than our parents, have as much contact with us while we are growing up than our teachers, and they are always trying to educate us.

Grandchild: So, would you name a teacher who made a difference in your life?

Grandpa: I don't think a teacher would be in my top five, although I encountered some great teachers.

Grandchild: Who would make your top five?

Grandpa: Number one would certainly be your grandma, and not only because we were together for 68 years. She was the positive optimist that I needed to help make my dreams come true. I would never have become a doctor without her encouragement, and probably not many other women would have agreed to have such a large family. I am a realist, and I like to know how things will turn out before I start. Your Grandma was a visionary, and she focused on the goal, not the journey. Pursuing a medical degree with eight children required a visionary because it was certainly not realistic.

Grandchild: Did anyone else influence you in your doctor dream?

Grandpa: I can think of two others. One was Dr. Worobec, who was a doctor in the TB Hospital, where I spent 15 months. He grew up in the Ukraine and suffered persecution from both the Nazis and the Communists before moving to this Country. I wrote a short biography about his challenging life while I was in the hospital, and he encouraged me to pursue my dream of becoming a doctor. It took me seven more years before I actually did that, but sometimes the impact of an encouraging word takes a while to blossom. The other person was Dr. Mayer, who was the Dean of Admissions at the University Of Missouri Medical School. When we went for my application interview, we connected. Who knows why we connect almost instantly with some people and not with others, but it happens. He was young, and I think he was intrigued by the challenge we were planning to take on. For some reason, he took a liking to us, put in a good word for me with the admissions committee and obtained much financial help for us during my time in medical school. He even hired a lawyer to help us with our zoning request challenge with the city, so Gloria could have a home beauty shop while I was in school.

Grandchild: Who else would put in your top five?

Grandpa: I would have to include my mother because I acquired many of her traits. She was not only a "people person", but she was also very much involved in her community. I like to think that I acquired those attributes from her.

Grandchild: Who was number five?

Grandpa: Number five is not so clear, so I will name two number fives. One was Dr. Smith, a colleague of mine in Hillsdale. I consider him my primary mentor during my medical practice. He was my OB consultant, and, since I delivered many babies, I called on him often. He was a great teacher and a very positive and uncritical consultant. Later in his career he went on to teach at two different medical schools. The other number five was Bruce McClain, a camping friend of mine when we were teenagers. I spent several summers with him when our families shared the same campground in Michigan's

	Upper Peninsula. We kept in touch through Christmas cards for 50 years.
Grandchild:	Did you ever let these people know what an influence they had on your life?
Grandpa:	You have touched on one of my regrets. Of these six, only my wife received adequate thanks. I actually made an attempt to reach out to two others. After 50 years of Christmas cards, I planned to visit Bruce in California when we were going to California to visit two of our children, but, when I called, his wife informed me that Bruce had just died. I had waited one month too long! I also tried to contact Dr. Worobec but found he had also passed away. Recently, a student from my teaching days nearly fifty years ago, contacted me to let me know that I had made a difference in his life. I didn't remember him, but I was both surprised and pleased. Why haven't I done that?
Grandchild:	I guess this time you are sharing with me an admission that you are still learning.
Grandpa:	We never stop learning the lessons of life. Let me leave you with two suggestions:

First of all, be aware of the impact you might have on other people. You never know when something you do or say will influence their lives. Try, always, to keep your influence a positive one.

Secondly, let people know if they have had a positive influence on your life – before it's too late. It is a message that never grows old and will always be appreciated. |
| Grandchild: | Thanks, Grandpa, and I want you to know that you have made a difference in my life. |
| Grandpa: | Thanks. That means a lot to me . . |

KILLING

Grandchild: Grandpa, do you think it is ever alright to kill someone – you know, the Ten Commandments and all?

Grandpa: What do you think?

Grandchild: I can think of one situation – self-defense. If someone is about to kill me, I think I would be justified in defending myself, even if it meant killing the other person.

Grandpa: I don't think you would get much argument there, although you might be criticized for using excessive or unwarranted force. It is easy, after the fact, to see other appropriate responses, but when a crisis occurs, you don't have the luxury of calm deliberation.

Grandchild: What about War. Isn't that a time when killing is warranted?

Grandpa: You will find people, of course, who oppose war, even when it appears to be the only option for protecting people and their possessions. I certainly don't like war – few people do - but I also come from a generation which was involved in a World War that was necessary to stop a tyrant from taking over the world. Had millions of Americans not been willing to go to war, the world would be quite different today. I think I would have to agree that killing during war becomes a necessary evil.

Grandchild: Is suffering ever a reason for ending a life?

Grandpa:	Sometimes we put animals out of their misery by killing them, and we feel this is humane. But should we do the same thing with humans?
Grandchild:	I think you are talking about euthanasia. I have difficulty with that issue.
Grandpa:	Why?
Grandchild:	Because it seems humane, sometimes, just like with animals, but it also appears to be the easy way out for family members. After the death they won't feel the obligation to provide help any more. It certainly is a dilemma.
Grandpa:	And it is one that many families struggle with.
Grandchild:	But suppose someone requests it?
Grandpa:	Why would the person request it?
Grandchild:	Maybe he or she is in a lot of pain.
Grandpa:	We have medications to control pain. Why not relieve the pain instead of ending a life?
Grandchild:	Maybe the person doesn't feel like there is any reason to live any more.
Grandpa:	Perhaps we can help him find a reason to live. People get depressed, but this is not a reason to end their lives, even if they request it. As you say, that is the simple solution – but not usually the best.
Grandchild:	Any other reasons for killing someone that are justified?
Grandpa:	Not that I can think of – unless you want to kill me for giving you so much advice.
Grandchild:	Not yet. Thanks, Grandpa.

LEADERSHIP

Grandchild: Grandpa, you and Grandma have been part of a number of different groups. What do you think are the most important characteristics of successful organizations?
Grandpa: That's a rather profound question.
Grandchild: I can be profound sometimes.
Grandpa: Sometimes.
Grandchild: OK, not often, but answer my question.
Grandpa: First of all, any worthwhile organization should have worthwhile objectives.
Grandchild: You mean, like good goals?
Grandpa: I think you understand. Without worthwhile goals, an organization will be unlikely to succeed, whether it is a business, a charitable group or a group of people promoting a cause.
Grandchild: You mean, a successful organization needs meaningful objectives.
Grandpa: Your wisdom sometimes amazes me.
Grandchild: Never mind the compliments. What else is required for a group to succeed?
Grandpa: Leadership.
Grandchild: What kind of leadership?
Grandpa: I think that there are two kinds of leadership that are important in a successful organization.
Grandchild: What are those?

Grandpa:	One is vision. You need someone who can focus on the goals rather than the journey. This usually is a person who is optimistic and doesn't get bogged down with the details of how the goal can be reached. Your Grandma was a good example of a visionary.
Grandchild:	What did she do that was visionary – besides having twelve children?
Grandpa:	She encouraged two local organizations to achieve goals they both originally considered unrealistic.
Grandchild:	What did they achieve?
Grandpa:	First of all, the Hillsdale Community Theatre owns their own theatre building, in part, because of her vision.
Grandchild:	How did that happen?
Grandpa:	Well, the building, an old movie theater that had quit showing films years before, was owned by the Village of Jonesville, and they decided to sell it. They appealed for bids. Your Grandma was on the HCT Board at the time, and she recommended the group submit a bid of $5,000. Other members of the Board reminded her that the organization didn't have any money. Her response was, "Don't worry about the money. We will raise it." She convinced a majority of the Board to support her, and the bid was submitted. It was accepted by the Village. Now, 47 years later, the organization has a beautiful debt-free performance venue in which to present their many wonderful yearly productions.
Grandchild:	So, the money got raised?
Grandpa:	Oh yes, but that required the efforts of the other important members of an organization – the trench workers.
Grandchild:	What in the world do you mean by "trench workers"?
Grandpa:	These are the people who actually dig the trench after the visionary promotes it. Seldom are the two the same person. You need both. Without a vision, nothing gets planned, but without the workers, no plan gets accomplished.
Grandchild:	What was the other project Grandma promoted?

Grandpa: The Alpha Omega Care Center.

Grandchild: What happened there?

Grandpa: Once again she encouraged the Board of that nonprofit organization to purchase a building in which they could offer their free support services to women and babies. Until that time, the group had provided these services in rented facilities. Once again, some of the other Board members complained that there was no money for such a purchase. However, her persistence paid off and today the organization provides these services in their own building. And, remarkably, more than half the mortgage has already been paid off. The trench workers, in this case, are the many volunteers who provide these services and the many donors who have supported the Center financially.

Grandchild: Are there any other visionaries in our family.

Grandpa: We have several visionaries, but we also have lots of trench workers. Our daughter, Terry, is a visionary, who will leave a lasting legacy in the community, the beautiful Perennial Park Senior Center. When she started work as the only fulltime employee at the Hillsdale Senior Center over two decades ago, limited services were provided from a small space in the basement of a church. Because of her vision and with the help of a lot of trench workers, multiple Senior services are now provided in a spacious new building with over 60 employees and hundreds of volunteers.

Grandchild: I would like to be a visionary and be the creator of something important, but I think I am probably just a trench worker.

Grandpa: So am I, but remember that trench workers are just as important as visionaries. We just fill a different role.

Grandchild: So your message today is that we need both visionaries and trench workers in order to accomplish great things.

Grandpa: You _were_ listening.

Grandchild: I always listen to your words of wisdom. Thanks, Grandpa.

⸮?⸮
LIFE

Grandchild: Grandpa, when do you think life begins?
Grandpa: That's a rather profound question from a young person.
Grandchild: Sometimes I can be profound, but don't get used to it.
Grandpa: When do YOU think life begins?
Grandchild: I thought I was asking the questions.
Grandpa: Sometimes I like to find out where your question is coming from before I answer.
Grandchild: OK, I guess I think that life begins at birth.
Grandpa: And what is it before birth?
Grandchild: Potential life.
Grandpa: Do you think we should protect a potential life, so it can become a life.
Grandchild: What do you mean?
Grandpa: If you cracked open an egg and found a dead chick instead of just egg white and egg yolk, how would you feel?
Grandchild: I'd feel like I picked the wrong egg. I was planning to eat an egg, not a chicken.
Grandpa: Was it a chicken before you cracked open the shell?
Grandchild: I don't think I like where this conversation is taking me.
Grandpa: Why not?
Grandchild: Because you're going to equate this to an unborn human.
Grandpa: What's the difference?
Grandchild: So you think we should protect a baby before it's born?

Grandpa: We protect eagles before birth. Do you know you can be arrested if you destroy an eagle's egg? I happen to think unborn humans are at least as valuable as unborn eagles.

Grandchild: You've backed me into one of you logical corners again.

Grandpa: Let's use a different approach. How would you describe a live human being?

Grandchild: Well, it should look like a human being, contain human organs, have a heart beat and have a brain so it could think.

Grandpa: You have just described a preborn baby.

Grandchild: But there is one other characteristic in my definition of a live human being. It should be able to function on its own.

Grandpa: You have just eliminated small children, the handicapped and the aged from the human race because they can't function on their own either. Their only additional qualification is that they have been born.

Grandchild: I hate it when this happens. You have used my own definition of human life to make me acknowledge that human life begins before birth.

Grandpa: You CAN be profound.

Grandchild: Or just dumb. Thanks, Grandpa.

LONGEVITY

Grandchild: Grandpa, why do you think you and Grandma have lived so long?

Grandpa: I think what you are saying is; "How did you get to be so old?"

Grandchild: That doesn't sound as nice as the way I said it.

Grandpa: It means the same thing, but it is a good question, even though I'm not sure I know the answer.

Grandchild: Don't you have any words of wisdom for us younger folks, so we can live a long time too?

Grandpa: Well, most importantly, choose your parents wisely.

Grandchild: Aw, come on, Grandpa, we can't choose our parents.

Grandpa: Too bad, because that is probably the most important factor in determining your life expectancy. If your parents lived to a ripe old age, then your chance of doing the same is pretty good.

Grandchild: OK, I'm stuck with my parent's genes. What can I do to increase my chances for bonus years?

Grandpa: You can make healthy lifestyle choices.

Grandchild: Here comes my Grandpa advice.

Grandpa: You asked the question.

Grandchild: Maybe I won't like the answer.

Grandpa: Then you shouldn't have asked the question. And if you don't listen, it won't make any difference anyway.

Grandchild: OK, Grandpa, you have my attention.

Grandpa: First I need to ask you if you <u>want</u> to live a long time.

Grandchild: Only if I can be as healthy as you when I reach the golden years.

Grandpa: For starters, you are over the first hurdle because you have been blessed with ancestors who have lived long lives, and chronic diseases like cancer and heart trouble are uncommon. I am also not aware of any Alzheimers in the family. So, if you die young, it is probably the result of something you do.

Grandchild: You are really putting the pressure on me, aren't you?

Grandpa: Don't you want to be in charge of your own health?

Grandchild: Sure, but then I will have to take responsibility for the outcome.

Grandpa: Your understanding amazes me.

Grandchild: OK, then what do you recommend I do?

Grandpa: Actually, it's what you don't do that will probably be most important if you want a long life.

Grandchild: You're going to talk to me about lifestyle, aren't you?

Grandpa: You are becoming remarkably perceptive.

Grandchild: OK, tell me what I shouldn't do.

Grandpa: I won't be telling you anything you don't already know, but that doesn't mean that in the future you will faithfully avoid all these things.

Grandchild: Let me hear your list before I decide if I like it.

Grandpa: My list is short. First of all, avoid dangerous activities that might result in life threatening outcomes. Secondly, avoid things that might become addicting and damage your mind and your body. Three obvious examples are smoking that damages the lungs, excessive alcohol intake that damages your liver and overeating that puts extra stress on the heart. Those three organs are critical in achieving longevity, so it's a good idea to take care of them. While the body has powerful healing powers, some damaged organs will never return to normal.

Grandchild: Well, you've told me what not to do. Are there things I should do to help me live longer?
Grandpa: I'm impressed that you are actually asking me for advice.
Grandchild: I <u>thought</u> you would like that.
Grandpa: Not sure what that response means, but I will share my thoughts, anyway.
Grandchild: I knew you would.
Grandpa: Sometimes I get the feeling that you are patronizing me because I'm so old.
Grandchild: Not sure what patronizing means, but I really do listen to your words of wisdom – honestly.
Grandpa: OK, I believe you. My to-do list is also short. Eat properly, exercise regularly, continue to have things to do and always have something to look forward to. It also helps to have someone to love.
Grandchild: You had Grandma.
Grandpa: Exactly. You really are perceptive.
Grandchild: I'm just perceiving what you pointed out. Thanks, Grandpa

LOVE

Grandchild: Grandpa, what is love?

Grandpa: Wow! That's a rather profound question for such a young person.

Grandchild: I can be profound sometimes.

Grandpa: Very seldom.

Grandchild: OK, so what are your thoughts about my profound question?

Grandpa: First of all, love is a word that has different meanings. There are many different types of love. The love of your mother, the love of your children, the love of your spouse, the love of your siblings, the love of a job, the love of a home, the love of a vacation spot, the love of God, etc.. We use the word "love" to express our affection for all of these, but they are not the same. Some are people related and some are object related, but we often use the same term of affection for both even though they are very different.

Grandchild: I certainly don't love my brothers and sisters like I love my mother. In fact there are times when I'm not sure I love my siblings at all.

Grandpa: I hope that feeling is only temporary. Your love for your mother, on the other hand, is, hopefully, quite constant.

Grandchild: Except when she won't let me do what I want to do.

Grandpa: You are confusing love with behavior.

Grandchild: What's the difference?

Grandpa: Love is how you feel toward something or some person, but behavior is how you express that feeling. They are not always compatible. Sometimes your actions do not properly convey your love. That's why people sometimes have problems in their marriages, or why people get fired from their jobs. You may say unkind things to someone you love, or you may not be a reliable employee at a job that you say you love.

Grandchild: Sounds like love is kind of optional.

Grandpa: Very much so. You have a choice as to what or who you love, and your choices are very much influenced by things that happen. Your love for a friend may be lost if the friend wrongs you in some way. Your love for a job may be compromised by a mean boss. And your love may also change from time to time. A mother's love for her newborn is different than her love when the child is five – and certainly is different when the child is a teenager because behavior has impacted her feelings. This doesn't mean she loves the child less; it just means that her love has lost some of its simplicity.

Grandchild: I don't think you are helping me by giving me a simple definition of love. It sounds much too complicated.

Grandpa: Alright, here's a simple definition. Love is wanting to do something nice for someone or something without expecting anything in return.

Grandchild: That's simple alright. Thanks, Grandpa.

MARRIAGE

Grandchild: Grandpa, can I ask you a question?
Grandpa: As long as it's not too hard.
Grandchild: Why did you marry Grandma?
Grandpa: Because I fell in love with her.
Grandchild: How did you know you were in love with her?
Grandpa: How did I know I loved her? That's a difficult question.
Grandchild: That's why I'm asking it.
Grandpa: Well, she was a lifeguard at our local swimming pool, and she was very pretty.
Grandchild: So, you married her because she was a pretty lifeguard?
Grandpa: Not really. She was only 16, and I was 21. There were a lot of pretty lifeguards.
Grandchild: So, why did you pick grandma?
Grandpa: I didn't right away. It took me three years to finally pop the question.
Grandchild: Why did it take you so long?
Grandpa: We were both quite young and busy going to school. She was just finishing high school and starting college, and I was going to college. However, several things happened during those three years.
Grandchild: What happened?
Grandpa: We both were "pinned" to other people.
Grandchild: What do you mean, "pinned"?

Grandpa: Well, on college campuses there was a tradition called "Pinning". It was kind of like "going steady". A boy would give his girl his fraternity pin to wear, to let people know that they were a couple. There was a ceremony at the girl's dorm where the guy's fraternity brothers would sing in front of the girl's dorm to celebrate the occasion. Since I was a Sigma Chi, the "Sweetheart of Sigma Chi" was the song we always sang. I was a senior by then and had never experienced such an occasion for myself. I was dating a cute co-ed on campus at that time, and, although we were not planning to get married, I wanted to experience a "pinning" before I graduated. Your Grandma, at about the same time, accepted a pin from her high school boyfriend, who was attending another college. So, we were both "pinned" to other people at the start of that summer.

Grandchild: So, how did you two get together?

Grandpa: Well, your Grandma's sister let me know that your Grandma had joined the Catholic Church, and since I was Catholic, this sparked a new interest. I called her and asked if we could talk about why she had joined the Catholic Church. She agreed, and we took a long walk up to the swimming pool and back. I asked her why she had joined the Church, but we also talked about our shared dream of having a large family. We had both read "Cheaper by the Dozen" and agreed that this sounded like an exciting goal.

Grandchild: You were both "pinned" to other people, and you were talking about having a large family?

Grandpa: To make our relationship even more unlikely, I was going away for the summer to work at a camp, so we didn't see each other again for several months. However, by the end of the summer we were planning our wedding.

Grandchild: How in the world did that happen?

Grandpa:	During the summer we wrote letters frequently, and we both became "un-pinned". I had written to your grandma that I had three things to discuss with her. I mentioned the first two but told her that the last one I would reveal when I saw her. I thought a little intrigue might make it more dramatic.
Grandchild:	So, what was the third thing?
Grandpa:	That I wanted to marry her.
Grandchild:	Wait a minute! You both started the summer in other relationships, didn't see each other for two months and then decided you should get married?
Grandpa:	Well, it didn't happen right away. Your grandma was still dating her old boyfriend. She was alternating dates with me and him for a couple of weeks, but then we realized we were in love, and before I left for graduate school that September, I had asked her parents for permission to marry her. I think they were in shock that things had changed so radically during that summer, but they did agree to my request.
Grandchild:	So, when did you get married?
Grandpa:	That's also an interesting story. We at first planned to get married the next August, but each time we saw each other, we moved the date up.
Grandchild:	Why did you do that?
Grandpa:	Well, in those days, we believed people should be married before they had children.
Grandchild:	What a novel idea.
Grandpa:	It works pretty well.
Grandchild:	Did you have birth control then:?
Grandpa:	We sure did. It was called "abstinence". It worked 100% of the time and had no side effects.
Grandchild:	Are you trying to tell me something?
Grandpa:	Only if you are willing to listen.
Grandchild:	I'm not sure I wanted to hear the message.
Grandpa:	Then you shouldn't have asked the question.

Grandchild: So when did you finally get married?

Grandpa: I was in school, remember, so we didn't see each other very often We saw each other at Thanksgiving and moved the date up to June. Then we saw each other at Christmas and moved the date to March. We would have moved it up further, but you can't have a Catholic Church wedding during Lent, so we decided to get married the day after Easter, a Monday.

Grandchild: You got married on a Monday!

Grandpa: A bit unusual, but it had several advantages. First of all, we didn't have to decorate the church. The Easter decorations were still in place. Secondly, we could send out lots of invitations because most people were working and couldn't attend on a Monday.

Grandchild: You and Grandma were married for 68 years. What was your secret?

Grandpa: Marry someone you love, overcome the challenges together and honor the commitment you make on your wedding day to stay married the rest of your life.

Grandchild: Thanks, Grandpa.

MEDICINE

Grandchild: Grandpa, has medicine changed much since you were a Doctor?
Grandpa: It has changed a great deal.
Grandchild: Has it gotten better or worse?
Grandpa: In some ways it has gotten better, but it some ways the changes have not been very beneficial.
Grandchild: How has it gotten better?
Grandpa: Well, with the new technology, doctors today have many more tools to use in order to make correct diagnoses, and new treatments have enabled today's Doctors to achieve better results. People are living healthier and longer now.
Grandchild: That is certainly good. What is not so good?
Grandpa: There are two parts of medicine. We used to call these the "science of medicine" and the "art of medicine".
Grandchild: What do you mean by the "art of medicine"?
Grandpa: Actually, this is not unique with the practice of medicine. It is present in most everything we do. You may have a skill in something, but the way you use that skill with people is equally important.
Grandchild: I don't think I understand.
Grandpa: Well, suppose, as a doctor, I decide what is the proper treatment for a patient's problem. That's the scientific part, but how I present that to the patient is the art of medicine and is equally important. If the patient does not

	feel comfortable with me or with my suggested treatment, my recommendation may not be accepted. So, a skilled doctor needs to be able to interact with a patient in an effective way in addition to knowing the right treatment.
Grandchild:	I think what you are saying is that communication skills are important in medicine.
Grandpa:	Actually, communication skills are important in most everything you do, whether you are a doctor, a lawyer, an accountant, a factory worker or a farmer.
Grandchild:	Do you think the art of medicine is not as good as it used to be?
Grandpa:	I'm probably biased because of my age, but I think the doctor-patient relationship was much closer when I was in practice than it is now.
Grandchild:	Why do you say that?
Grandpa:	For one thing, most people today have a number of different doctors – a different one for each ailment. The Family Doctor, who took care of your medical needs from birth till death, with occasional help from specialists, is a thing of the past. Medicine has become much more specialized today. When a patient of mine needed hospitalization, I took care of him during his hospital stay. Now, a "hospitalist" takes care of him while he's hospitalized. If a patient requires intensive care, an "intensive care specialist" takes over his care. And when that patient returns to the care of his family doctor after leaving the hospital, the family doc may or may not have a report on his hospital care before he next sees him in the office. The specialist focuses on the acute problem, while the family doc is concerned about long term care.
Grandchild:	Won't he get better care if a specialist takes care of him?
Grandpa:	Perhaps, but the specialist doesn't know him as well as the patient's family physician, so his treatment may not take into consideration his family, his living environment or other life challenges he may have.

Grandchild: Sounds like you're lamenting the loss of "The Good Old Days"

Grandpa: I suppose you're right. We old timers will always think things were better when we were in charge. But remember that I <u>am</u> a member of the Greatest Generation.

Grandchild: That's true. Thanks, Grandpa.

MONEY

Grandchild: Grandpa, are you wealthy?
Grandpa: You mean do I have a lot of money?
Grandchild: Yes
Grandpa: Then my answer would have to be "No".
Grandchild: But you were a doctor. Aren't all doctors wealthy?
Grandpa: Not this one.
Grandchild: How were you able to support such a large family?
Grandpa: I'm not sure. Creative financing, I guess.
Grandchild: What do you mean by creative financing?
Grandpa: It means doing what's necessary to not spend more money than you have.
Grandchild: I hope I make a lot of money, so I won't have to worry about spending too much.
Grandpa: That's not the way it works for 99% of people. That's a mistake many people make.
Grandchild: What do you mean?
Grandpa: Financial security is not usually achieved by having more money. Rich people can also have financial difficulties because of spending too much. Financial security is achieved by learning to control your spending regardless of how much you make. If you don't learn to control your spending when you have a little money, you probably won't control it when you have a lot.
Grandchild: So how do you control spending?

Grandpa:	Well, it's wise to set some money aside each month in a savings account before you pay your bills. If you pay your bills first, you will probably never have anything left for savings.
Grandchild:	But suppose I don't have enough to pay all my bills if I save first?
Grandpa:	Then, it's probably time to find a way to reduce your bills.
Grandchild:	Did you do that when you were supporting your family?
Grandpa:	I did a couple of things to help me set limits on how much I could spend. First of all, I paid myself a set salary from my medical practice, so I knew how much I could spend. Since it was my practice, I could have just taken money as I needed it, but then it would have been too easy to overspend if there was extra money available. That's not the way successful businesses work. I needed a specified income budget for myself so I knew how much I could spend..
Grandchild:	What else did you do?
Grandpa:	I set up three savings accounts into which I deposited a small amount each payday.
Grandchild:	Why three accounts?
Grandpa:	One was for vacations, one was for Christmas and one was kind of an emergency account for unexpected expenses. Even though the deposits were not very large, it is surprising how the money accumulates, and, when vacations, Christmas or emergencies occurred, I had some money set aside.
Grandchild:	I think you are telling me that I should save some money.
Grandpa:	You are very observant, and you should start right away. Don't wait until you have "extra" money, because that time will probably never arrive. You will always find a way to spend it.
Grandchild:	Any other financial advice?
Grandpa:	Don't use credit cards as loan agencies.
Grandchild:	You mean I shouldn't use a credit card?

Grandpa: That's not what I mean. Today a credit card is almost a necessity, and it does have one advantage.

Grandchild: What is that?

Grandpa: It provides a nice way to keep track of your spending, and, if you pay off your credit card each month it doesn't cost you a thing.

Grandchild: So, what's the problem with a credit card?

Grandpa: If you don't pay it off each month, it will be like taking out a loan with a very high interest rate. Many people simply make the minimum payment each month and don't pay any attention to how much they are paying in interest. Credit card companies stay in business because most people don't pay off their balance each month.

Grandchild: You mean if everyone paid off their cards each month, the companies wouldn't make a profit?

Grandpa: Congratulations. You are expressing a bit of wisdom.

Grandchild: Thanks for the compliment.

Grandpa: For most of us, having enough money will always be a challenge, but if money is the only measure of your happiness, then you are focusing on the wrong thing. Money, alone, is not going to produce a happy marriage, a loving family, close friendships or a meaningful life. Manage your finances well, but don't let money dominate your life. I have never been wealthy, but I have been very blessed with many meaningful relationships. I would not trade these relationships for wealth.

Grandchild: Thanks, Grandpa.

MORALITY

Grandchild:	Grandpa, what is morality?
Grandpa:	How did you come up with such a profound question?
Grandchild:	I'm not sure I even know what profound means.
Grandpa:	So - why the sudden interest in morality?
Grandchild:	Because one of my teachers said that morality is important.
Grandpa:	And did your teacher say why it is important?
Grandchild:	She said that morality is what makes us human. She said that other forms of life do not have morality.
Grandpa:	Sounds like your teacher is rather wise.
Grandchild:	But what is morality?
Grandpa:	Quite simply, it is the rightness or wrongness of an action.
Grandchild:	So, morality can be good or bad?
Grandpa:	Well, actually, to be moral is to be good. To be immoral is to be bad.
Grandchild:	How do I know if I am moral or immoral?
Grandpa:	Do you know when you do something good?
Grandchild:	Usually
Grandpa:	How do you know?
Grandchild:	I feel better for having done it.
Grandpa:	Do you know when you do something bad?
Grandchild:	Yes
Grandpa:	How do you know?
Grandchild:	I feel guilty because I know what I did was wrong.

Grandpa:	Do you ever do something even when you know it's wrong?
Grandchild:	I'm afraid I am guilty of that sometimes.
Grandpa:	Morality is choosing to do the right thing, even when it is difficult. I think it is safe to say that none of us are perfectly moral. We all probably make immoral decisions sometimes.
Grandchild:	You mean we knowingly choose to something immoral? Why would we do that?
Grandpa:	Suppose you are seeking a job, and you are in competition with a friend who told you, in confidence, something he had done that would probably disqualify him from the job.you both are seeking. Would you tell the employer?
Grandchild:	If I did, I would probably get the job.
Grandpa:	But how would you feel about it?
Grandchild:	I guess I would feel like I had betrayed my friend, so I probably wouldn't tell.
Grandpa:	Suppose that you are really desperate for this job in order to support your three small children and your handicapped wife who is unable to work. Your friend is much better off financially than you, is not married and has no one else depending on him for support.
Grandchild:	You are making this decision awfully difficult. Under those circumstances I might reveal the information by telling myself that the employer really should be informed before he decides who to hire, or, perhaps, by rationalizing that my need for the job is much greater than my friend's.
Grandpa:	Morality is sometimes difficult to maintain. We will make many decisions in our lives, and will sometimes be faced with choices that test our morality. Usually we know what the right decision is, but circumstances may encourage us to do something we know, deep down, is not right.

Grandchild: Sounds like circumstances will play a big part in how moral a person I am.
Grandpa: Not really. Your choices will determine your morality. Circumstances will simply reveal it.
Grandchild: I guess you're saying that my morality is up to me. I can't blame my immorality on my circumstances. .
Grandpa: Once again, I am amazed at your wisdom.
Grandchild: I'm learning. Thanks, Grandpa.

OPINIONS

Grandchild: Grandpa, are you opinionated?
Grandpa: I do have opinions. What do you mean by opinionated?
Grandchild: I mean, do have strong opinions about things and won't listen to other people's opinions?
Grandpa: Do you mean not listen to them or not agree with them?
Grandchild: What's the difference?
Grandpa: I like to think that I am willing to listen to other's opinions even though sometimes I may not agree with them. What about you?
Grandchild: I'm supposed to be asking the questions. I'm just wondering how you respond to people with whom you don't agree.
Grandpa: That depends a lot on the attitude of the other person.
Grandchild: What do you mean?
Grandpa: If the other person is willing to engage in a real discussion and a sharing of opinions, it would make me more likely to do the same. But if the person is simply interested in proclaiming his opinion without engaging in any real discussion, then I probably would not be very interested in continuing the conversation.
Grandchild: How can you tell if he is interested in a real discussion?
Grandpa: There is one criteria by which you can determine whether a rational discussion can take place.
Grandchild: And what is that?

Grandpa: You have to start from a point where you both agree.
Grandchild: What do you mean?
Grandpa: If you can't find a starting point on a topic where you have agreement, it is not likely that the discussion is going to be productive.
Grandchild: Can you give me an example?
Grandpa: Suppose you and I disagree on the benefits of welfare programs. You may feel that the government should provide more benefits, and I may feel that government welfare just makes people lazy and too dependent on government help. In order to have a reasonable discussion on the topic, we must have a starting point at which we both agree.
Grandchild: What could that be?
Grandpa: Perhaps we could agree that people in this Country should not starve and should have a place to live. From that agreement we might have disagreements about how to achieve this, but at least we would have the same objective. If you can't find a starting point of agreement, the discussion will not be productive.
Grandchild: It seems like today, people don't follow this process very well. They just want to proclaim their beliefs without much interest in discussing them.
Grandpa: Unfortunately, that is often the case – especially in politics. People too often simply follow YWAFWYALF.
Grandchild: What in the world does that mean?
Grandpa: You will always find what you are looking for.
Grandchild: I'm still not sure I understand.
Grandpa: We all have opinions about people, places, political parties and programs, and we find reasons to support our beliefs.
Grandchild: Is that bad?
Grandpa: Not bad. It's human nature. Everyone does it. We all try to justify our beliefs. For instance, if we like someone, we will find reasons that we like them. If we dislike

someone, we find reasons to dislike them. Our reasons are not always logical or even correct, but we use them anyway. This is especially true in politics. We find reasons to support our political party and reasons to criticize the other party and rational discussions are difficult because our opinions are so entrenched.

Grandchild: I guess that's why politicians can't accomplish much. They can't agree on a starting point.

Grandpa: Hooray! You understand. There is hope for the future,

Grandchild: Not unless my generation can find the starting point! Thanks, Grandpa.

PERSONALITY FLAWS

Grandchild: Grandpa, why are some people more likeable than others?
Grandpa: If I could answer that, I could give you a formula for making yourself likeable.
Grandchild: Sounds like a good idea. Why don't you do that?
Grandpa: Because likeability is not so easy to define, and what some people find likeable is not always the same as what other people find likeable. I guess this is why we have different friends and why we choose to associate with different people.
Grandchild: You mean likeability is not the same for everyone.
Grandpa: Not only is it not the same for everyone, but it is not always the same for each individual.
Grandchild: What do you mean?
Grandpa: Well, do you use the same criteria for everyone you come in contact with?
Grandchild: You mean, do I judge everyone the same?
Grandpa: Do you?
Grandchild: I think I try to.
Grandpa: Let me approach this from a different direction. Do you think all of your friends are perfect?
Grandchild: Oh no, but I also have flaws, so why should I expect them to be perfect.
Grandpa: Do any of them do things that annoy you?

Grandchild:	Oh yes. Billy has a bad habit of interrupting conversations, in which he is not a part, and Bobby, my roommate, is sloppy and never cleans up his messes.
Grandpa:	But you still like them.
Grandchild:	Sure, because they are both a lot of fun to be around.
Grandpa:	Would you want to spend time with someone who had those irritating traits but was not fun to be around?
Grandchild:	Probably not, and those traits would probably be far more irritating.
Grandpa:	So, with some people, you ignore their bad habits because they have some offsetting good points.
Grandchild:	I never thought of it that way, but I guess you're right.
Grandpa:	I'm recording that in my record book – the one time you thought I was right.
Grandchild:	Don't get used to it.
Grandpa:	I will cherish the moment.
Grandchild:	So, what is your theory about why we like some people and not others?
Grandpa:	Not sure I can answer that to your total satisfaction, but let me try.

We all use different criteria by which to judge people, and, since none of us is perfect, we often have to balance a person's good and bad traits to decide whether we like them or not. Let me give you a couple of examples.

The first time we met a future grandson-in-law was when he came over to have dinner with us. After we had finished eating, he got up, without being asked, and cleared all the dirty dishes and took them to the kitchen. This action immediately bonded him with my wife and offset any unpleasant traits he might have had.

Another example: One of our sons is annoyingly boisterous and opinionated, but his financial advice helped us to remain financially solvent in our declining years, so we like him and try to ignore his annoying habits. Of course, he is our son, so we can't disown him!

None of us is without some personality blemish, so we often find ourselves choosing people as our friends in spite of their blemishes. This is probably a good thing because it also works in the other direction. Some people may choose to befriend us in spite of <u>our</u> blemishes.

Grandchild: Thanks, Grandpa. Glad to know I don't have to be perfect to be your favorite grandchild.

PLANNED PARENTHOOD

Grandchild: Grandpa, why don't you like Planned Parenthood?
Grandpa: Because they kill babies.
Grandchild: I thought they helped women who were pregnant.
Grandpa: That's what they want you to believe, but one out of every eight women who enter a Planned Parenthood facility ends up with an abortion. Since many women are not pregnant when they go there; they just want Pap smears, STD tests or breast exams, the percentage of pregnant women who visit Planned Parenthood and end up with an abortion is much higher than one in eight.
Grandchild: But I heard that abortions make up only 3% of Planned Parenthood's services.
Grandpa: Planned Parenthood is quite clever. They use the 3% figure to obscure how many abortions they actually do. They produce this number by including every service a patient receives as a separate service. A patient, in addition to having an abortion, may also have a pregnancy test, STD screening and may receive birth control pills. Planned Parenthood counts each of these for statistical purposes. That's how they arrive at the 3% figure.
Grandchild: You mean their statistics are misleading?
Grandpa: Exactly. In their most recent Annual Report for 2015-1016, Planned Parenthood performed 328,348 abortions. This was about 30% of all abortions performed that year

	in this Country. This means that every day 897 unborn babies were killed that year by Planned Parenthood abortionists.
Grandchild:	But don't they provide other services to help women?
Grandpa:	Sure, but the same Annual Report showed that Cancer Screenings, Pap Tests, Breast exams and prenatal services all decreased significantly from the previous year while abortions increased. And to make things worse, we taxpayers are forced to support Planned Parenthood. Over 500 million dollars, about 50% of their income, comes from our tax dollars.
Grandchild:	I thought Planned Parenthood was a non-profit organization. Why should they be supported by tax money?
Grandpa:	An excellent question, and some of our conservative legislators are asking the same thing.
Grandchild:	If a woman didn't want an abortion but wanted the other services, where would she go if Planned Parenthood wasn't around?
Grandpa:	Another good question. We have thousands of Women's Care Centers around the Country that provide many of those services free, don't do abortions, are supported by private donations and receive no government funds. Our own Alpha Omega Center, here in Hillsdale, is one of those places.
Grandchild:	Why don't we use our tax money for those places rather than Planned Parenthood?
Grandpa:	You are full of wise questions today. Some of our legislators are trying to do just that.
Grandchild:	I understand now why you don't like Planned Parenthood. Thanks Grandpa.

POPULARITY

Grandchild: Grandpa, were you popular when you were growing up?
Grandpa: What do you mean by "popular"?
Grandchild: Well, did your classmates like you?
Grandpa: I had a group of friends who, I think, liked me. I don't know that this made me popular. Everybody has a few friends who like them.
Grandchild: Why did you choose your friends?
Grandpa: Oftentimes it was because we had similar interests – like sports or hobbies, but I think there is another reason that is hard to explain.
Grandchild: What is that?
Grandpa: Have you ever met someone for the first time and felt right away that it was someone you enjoyed talking with?
Grandchild: You mean like "love at first sight".
Grandpa: I'm not talking about a romantic attraction I'm just talking about the fact that I find some people more relatable than others. When I first meet them, some people just are more interesting to me. We connect. Others I have little interest in spending time with.
Grandchild: Why the difference?
Grandpa: It is, sometimes, because we agree on some topic, but often the connection exists before we even know the other's beliefs. I can't really explain it, but I don't think

	I'm unique. I think many people form friendships after very brief encounters.
Grandchild:	What does that have to do with popularity?
Grandpa:	I think that people who are considered popular have the ability to "connect" with a lot of other people.
Grandchild:	What should I do to be popular?
Grandpa:	Perhaps a better way to approach this is to ask yourself, "Who should I be to be popular?"
Grandchild:	What do you mean?
Grandpa:	Who you are is something you can control. What you do is just a reflection of who you are.
Grandchild:	You mean my behavior defines me?
Grandpa:	I think you are getting the message.
Grandchild:	There you go again – weaving one of life's lessons into your answers.
Grandpa:	You asked the question, didn't you?
Grandchild:	I guess I did. Thanks, Grandpa

PREJUDICE

Grandchild: Grandpa, can I ask you a question.
Grandpa: Of course, I have lots of answers if you ask the right questions.
Grandchild: Are you a prejudiced person?
Grandpa: Do you mean do I have a bias against certain people without good reason?
Grandchild: Yeah, I guess that's what I mean.
Grandpa: I hope not, but I am judgmental.
Grandchild: What's the difference?
Grandpa: Well, prejudice is related to who people are; judgmental is related to what people do.
Grandchild: Not sure I understand the difference.
Grandpa: Think of it this way: you don't have any choice about your parents, your ethnicity or the color of your skin, but you do have control over your behavior and how you treat other people. So, if someone is critical of you because of the things over which you have no control, they are being prejudiced, but if they criticize you for something you have done, they are being judgmental.
Grandchild: So, it's alright to be judgmental?
Grandpa: Even Jesus Christ was judgmental, but he judged people by what they did, not by who they were. The problem is that we don't always distinguish well between judgement and prejudice.

Grandchild: Maybe I should just not do either.
Grandpa: That's a noble goal, but it won't work.
Grandchild: Why not?
Grandpa: Do you think you should like everyone equally?
Grandchild: I think you are trying to lead me into one of your logical traps.
Grandpa: Just trying to help clarify your thought process.
Grandchild: OK, I admit that I don't like everyone the same.
Grandpa: Which simply means that you are judgmental about who you want as friends.
Grandchild: Is that bad?
Grandpa: Not bad, just a reality. We are all judgmental. Now let me ask you a question.
Grandchild: I don't think I'm going to like where you are taking me. OK, what's the question?
Grandpa: Is it ever right to dislike someone because of a group they are in?
Grandchild: Wouldn't that be prejudice?
Grandpa: Perhaps
Grandchild: When would it not be prejudice?
Grandpa: Suppose you had a friend who joined a gang that destroyed property, committed robberies and harmed other people. Would you continue to be his friend?
Grandchild: I can't imagine any friend of mine being so stupid, but, no, our friendship would be over.
Grandpa: You are now judging him by the group he joined. Is that prejudice?
Grandchild: No, I'm judging him by the choice he made to join that group. I don't think that's prejudice.
Grandpa: Very good. I think you now understand the difference between being prejudiced and being judgmental.
Grandchild: You mean I finally reached a correct understanding?
Grandpa: And what is that understanding?

Grandchild: That it's alright to be judgmental about what people do, but it's not alright to be prejudiced because of who people are.
Grandpa: Your understanding amazes me.
Grandchild: I'm afraid you are easily amazed. I'm not even sure what I understand. Anyway, thanks, Grandpa.

PRO-LIFE

Grandchild: You're pro-life, aren't you, Grandpa?
Grandpa: Aren't you?
Grandchild: What do you mean?
Grandpa: Well, don't you believe that every life has value?
Grandchild: Yes, but some lives are more valuable than others.
Grandpa: In what way?
Grandchild: Some people contribute more to the world than others.
Grandpa: How is that?
Grandchild: Some people have big businesses and provide jobs for a lot of people, some people are more talented and provide us with great entertainment, and some people are smarter and invent or build things that make our lives easier. Wouldn't you agree that they are more valuable?
Grandpa: What about the rest of us? Do we have value?
Grandchild: I hope so. Otherwise, I wouldn't be necessary.
Grandpa: What about a baby? How valuable is a baby?
Grandchild: I guess we won't know until he or she grows up.
Grandpa: So, we need to protect a baby until we see how valuable it is when it grows up?
Grandchild: Of course.
Grandpa: What if he or she turns out not to be very valuable from your perspective?
Grandchild: I think you are trying to back me into one of your logical corners.

Grandpa:	Just trying to establish how your value system relates to the Right To Life.
Grandchild:	What do you mean?.
Grandpa:	Well, do you think your right to live is dependent on how valuable you are?
Grandchild:	I sure hope not, because I don't feel very valuable right now.
Grandpa:	So what should qualify you for the right to live?
Grandchild:	Now, I am really in the corner. I guess I would say that if you are alive, you have the right to life.
Grandpa:	What if you haven't yet been born?
Grandchild:	Then you aren't alive.
Grandpa:	Why aren't you alive? Your heart is beating, your brain waves are functioning, and an ultrasound will show that you look like a tiny baby. The only differences are your size and your location.
Grandchild:	But an unborn baby is not independent. It can't function on its own.
Grandpa:	And a newborn can? Or a toddler? Or a six year old?
Grandchild:	Of course not, but an unborn baby is different. It hasn't breathed on its own yet.
Grandpa:	So, breathing on your own is your criteria for the right to live?
Grandchild:	Well, you have to admit that breathing is a significant difference between the born and unborn.
Grandpa:	What about adults who are on oxygen? They can't breathe on their own either.
Grandchild:	But they once did.
Grandpa:	So, once you take your first breath you have the right to life?
Grandchild:	I guess so.
Grandpa:	You aren't sure?
Grandchild:	Not really.
Grandpa:	An unborn child has not taken its first breath. Should it have the right to live?

Grandchild: You sure come up with some troubling questions.

Grandpa: Let me ask you something. If you fell in the lake and people rescued you but weren't sure whether you were alive or dead, would you want them to try to save you because you might be alive?

Grandchild: Of course.

Grandpa: Maybe unborn babies are like that. If you can't decide whether they are really alive, perhaps you should protect them in case they are.

Grandchild: Oh, Grandpa, you somehow always make me think of things differently.

Grandpa: Is that bad?

Grandchild: Not bad, just frustrating sometimes.

Grandpa: Maybe it's good to be frustrated sometimes.

Grandchild: If you say so. Thanks Grandpa.

PROTESTS

Grandchild: Grandpa, what do you think about protests?
Grandpa: What do you mean by protests?
Grandchild: Well, it's when you don't like something, and you protest it.
Grandpa: You mean like marching with large signs that announce what you're protesting?
Grandchild: Or maybe getting together with a large crowd in a park or in front of a building.
Grandpa: I don't oppose protests, as long as they are peaceful. Our Constitution gives us the right to protest, but, unfortunately, all protests aren't peaceful. Sometimes they cause damage to property or people. I don't approve of that.
Grandchild: Did you ever participate in a protest?
Grandpa: I once walked in the March For Life in Washington, D.C..
Grandchild: What were you protesting?
Grandpa: We were protesting abortion and promoting life.
Grandchild: Was it peaceful.
Grandpa: Oh yes. Even though a hundred thousand people from all over the Country took part, there was no damage to property and no one was injured. In fact, some of the participants even cleaned up all the trash after the March was over.
Grandchild: Why do protesters sometimes break windows and steal things?

Grandpa: I don't know. It seems to me that this would damage their reputation and make people less likely to support them.
Grandchild: Then why do they do it?
Grandpa: I think that often some of the protesters are just hoodlums. They don't really care what the protest is about. They just use the protest as an excuse for breaking the law, stealing things and causing damage. They hope they won't be prosecuted because they will be lost in the crowd.
Grandchild: Then they really are criminals.
Grandpa: They are, and they should be prosecuted.
Grandchild: Why aren't they?
Grandpa: Sometimes they are, but it may be difficult to identify the hoodlums in the crowd, and, if they are prosecuted, some people may complain that they are being prosecuted for protesting, not for causing damage. Law enforcement officials have a difficult job. They need to keep the peace but not appear to be interfering with free speech.
Grandchild: So even if you don't agree with someone, you would not interfere with their protests?
Grandpa: Not if the protests are peaceful, and as long as they don't interfere with <u>my</u> right to protest.
Grandchild: Instead of having protests, why don't people just sit down and talk about their differences?
Grandpa: That would be a great idea, but it wouldn't get the headlines that protestors are looking for. People want attention when they protest, and media outlets, unfortunately, are eager to publicize misbehavior. A quiet discussion might accomplish more, but it wouldn't make the exciting news that a law-breaking protest rally would.
Grandchild: Do protest rallies work?
Grandpa: Well, they do get lots of attention, and they might change some people's opinions. The protestors hope so. However, if they are not peaceful, they might just make people angry. If you do not agree with the protest in the first

	place, then violence and destruction will probably make you disagree more.
Grandchild:	I think I will only participate in peaceful protests. I don't like violence.
Grandpa:	Sounds like a wise decision.
Grandchild:	Thanks, Grandpa.

RICH & POOR

Grandchild: Grandpa, why do we have rich people and poor people?
Grandpa: What do you mean?
Grandchild: Well, some people have lots of money and other people have very little. It doesn't seem fair.
Grandpa: What would you suggest?
Grandchild: If we distributed all the money evenly, then everybody would probably have plenty.
Grandpa: And who would do this distributing?
Grandchild: Couldn't we all just agree to share the money equally?
Grandpa: Who would make sure that this sharing was done properly?
Grandchild: The government, I guess.
Grandpa: You have just described Socialism.
Grandchild: Is that bad?
Grandpa: It's been tried many times, and it has never worked.
Grandchild: Why not?
Grandpa: Let me ask you a question. Have you ever had a paying job?
Grandchild: Yes, in the summer I mow lawns and in the Fall I rake leaves.
Grandpa: Do you get paid for this?
Grandchild: Of course.
Grandpa: Would you do it if you didn't get paid?
Grandchild: Not unless I was doing it for you and grandma.

ASK GRANDPA

Grandpa: Do you have a friend who doesn't work during the Summer?

Grandchild: My friend, Bobby, doesn't work in the summer. He goes on vacations with his family.

Grandpa: Do you think you should share your Summer earnings with Bobby?

Grandchild: Why should I do that? I work hard for my money. Why should he get part of my earnings?

Grandpa: You have just described the problem with Socialism. In our Country the harder you work, the more money you earn, and you don't have to share it with the non-worker.

Grandchild: That make sense, but why are some people so wealthy?

Grandpa: Maybe they worked harder.

Grandchild: Maybe they were just lucky. Maybe they won the lottery and got a million dollars.

Grandpa: And where do you think that million dollars came from?

Grandchild: The people that run the lottery, I guess.

Grandpa: No, it came from the million people who bought a lottery ticket and didn't win. Very few people get rich from the lottery.

Grandchild: I suppose you're right. Well, how do people get rich, then?

Grandpa: I hate to break this to you, but most people get rich by working very hard.

Grandchild: Suppose I had a wonderful new idea, and it became an overnight success.

Grandpa: There aren't many overnight successes. Even good ideas require a lot of effort to become profitable.

Grandchild: So, you think it's ok for some people to have a lot more money than other people?

Grandpa: Let me tell you the story of one very successful person, Colonel Sanders. You are familiar with Kentucky Fried Chicken, I suppose.

Grandchild: Of course. There are Kentucky Fried Chicken places all around the Country. Colonel Sanders must have been very wealthy.

Grandpa: He was when he died, but when Colonel Sanders was 60 years old, the restaurant he owned was closed because the turnpike needed his land. He was out of business, but he thought people might be interested in his fried chicken recipe, so he started across the Country trying to get someone to try it. He called on a thousand people before he found someone who said he would try it. This was the beginning of his very profitable fried chicken franchise business. Do you think he was lucky?

Grandchild: He had to call on a thousand people, and he was 60 years old?

Grandpa: That's right.

Grandchild: I wouldn't call that lucky. He certainly worked very hard for his success.

Grandpa: And this is true of most successful people.

Grandchild: Were you ever wealthy, Grandpa?

Grandpa: Not if you measure wealth only by money. But if you measure wealth by happiness and having a loving family, I am very wealthy. Money is only one form of wealth and it is not the most important one.

Grandchild: Thanks, Grandpa.

SAVING

Grandchild: Grandpa, were you a saver?
Grandpa: What do you mean by "a saver"?
Grandchild: Well, did you try to save some money when you were working?
Grandpa: It took me a long time to learn how, but yes I did try to save.
Grandchild: I would like to be a saver, but I never seem to have any money left after I buy the things I want.
Grandpa: That's not the way to save.
Grandchild: What do you mean?
Grandpa: If you spend first, you will never have anything left to save.
Grandchild: But what if I save first and then don't have enough to pay my bills?
Grandpa: Then you will need to trim your expenses and make sure that savings are part of your budget. Have you ever had to not buy something because you didn't have enough money?
Grandchild: Of course.
Grandpa: How did you decide what not to buy?
Grandchild: I decided what was most important, and what I could do without.
Grandpa: That's what we call financial planning. You decide how much money you have and then decide what you will

spend it on. Savings should be number one on that list – or, perhaps, should come right after charitable contributions. After that, you can start making purchases with what is left.

Grandchild: I probably won't have enough left to make all the purchases I want to.

Grandpa: Join the club. That is true of most of us, so we have to decide which purchases are most important.

Grandchild: If I just had more money, I would have enough to save.

Grandpa: Wrong. You have just fallen into the financial pit that many people live in. The art of saving is not related to how much you make. If you don't learn to save when your income is small, you probably won't save when your income is big. It is the attitude of saving before you spend that is important – not the amount of your income. You can save more when you earn more, but not if you haven't adopted the attitude of saving. You will always find more things to buy if you have more money, so there is not likely to be any left over for saving.

Grandchild: Did you save when you were raising your big family?

Grandpa: Not at first, but several things encouraged me to save.

Grandchild: What were those?

Grandpa: Well, Christmas was not a happy time for me because I suddenly felt obligated to buy presents for my wife and all our children, and I had to spend money I didn't have. Secondly, I believed family vacations were important, and I didn't have the money to pay for them. Thirdly, when an emergency occurred, I didn't have the money set aside to handle it.

Grandchild: So, what did you do?

Grandpa: I established three savings accounts. One was for Christmas, one was for Vacations, and the other was for emergencies. I put a small amount in each account every payday before I paid my bills. When Christmas came I

Grandchild:	had money set aside, and the same was true for vacations. Emergencies were also less financially stressful.
Grandchild:	And you were still able to pay your bills?
Grandpa:	Oh yes, the bills got paid. The strange thing about saving before you spend is that after a while you don't miss the money you put in savings. You just plan your spending differently. If you were making $100 a week, and I told you that from now on you will only get $90, what would you do?
Grandchild:	I suppose I would plan to spend $90 instead of $100.
Grandpa:	And at the end of a year, you would have your bills paid and you would have $520 in your savings account.
Grandchild:	Wow! That would be awesome. Thanks, Grandpa. I think I will start saving.

SCHOOL

Grandchild: Grandpa, you went to a lot of school, didn't you?
Grandpa: I sure did.
Grandchild: You must have liked going to school.
Grandpa: Not really..
Grandchild: Then why did you spend so much time in school?
Grandpa: Because I wanted to be a doctor, and if you want to be a doctor, you have to spend a lot of time in school.
Grandchild: You must have been very smart.
Grandpa: Not really. I was an average student. I studied hard to get B's. People who spend a lot of time in school probably do it for one of three reasons.
Grandchild: And what are those?
Grandpa: The first reason is that some people simply enjoy the satisfaction and recognition of displaying their intelligence by getting good grades. They actually enjoy going to school. Others just want to accumulate a lot of knowledge, and they are the ones who usually do a lot of reading, too. And the final group are those, like me, who need lots of schooling to prepare for their chosen career.
Grandchild: So, you didn't like school?
Grandpa: I wouldn't say I didn't like it. I just had to work very hard at it, and I envied people who could get good grades without much study. Some people are better test takers than others, and this produces better grades.

Grandchild: Do you think I should go to college?
Grandpa: That depends on what you want to do.
Grandchild: I really don't know what I want to do.
Grandpa: Then why would you go to college.
Grandchild: To find out what I want to do.
Grandpa: That's an expensive way to make a decision. College education costs a lot.
Grandchild: So, how do I find out what I want to do?
Grandpa: How about getting a job?
Grandchild: You mean going to work right after high school?
Grandpa: Jobs can be great learning experiences, and going to work doesn't mean you can't still go to college.
Grandchild: But that would put me behind my classmates who are already in college.
Grandpa: That depends on your definition of "behind". Financially, you would be ahead. You would be earning money while they were acquiring debt.
Grandchild: But they would be a year closer to their chosen career.
Grandpa: You said you didn't yet have a career goal. Spending money at school trying to figure that out doesn't seem like a very wise choice. Working at a job not only provides you with an income, but it also gives you a taste of the real world. Oftentimes, this provides the incentive to seriously pursue a different career path. Education would then be more focused and profitable.
Grandchild: Suppose I don't want to go to college.
Grandpa: Then you shouldn't go. There are many excellent careers that don't require a college education. The building trades offer wonderful opportunities and, usually, you can earn money while learning, so you don't end up with a big school debt.
Grandchild: What if I decide I want to be a lawyer?
Grandpa: Then prepare to spend a lot of time in the classroom.
Grandchild: Maybe I just want to make lots of money.

Grandpa: That's not a career choice. I don't think you can major in Getting Rich. No career will guarantee that. I was a doctor and most doctors make a pretty good income, but that wasn't why I became a doctor, and I never made a lot of money. Of course, with twelve children to raise, "a lot of money" is a relative term.

Grandchild: So, do you think I should go to college?

Grandpa: Not my decision. That's for you to decide. In this Country you have plenty of options.

Grandchild: As usual, you ask questions rather than giving me answers. I guess that's a good thing. Thanks, Grandpa

SERVANT HEART

Grandchild: Grandpa, what do you mean when you say someone has a servant heart?

Grandpa: You heard me talking about who in our family has a servant heart, didn't you?

Grandchild: Yes, but I didn't hear my name mentioned.

Grandpa: Do you think you have a servant heart?

Grandchild: I guess I would have to know what it means first.

Grandpa: Probably a good observation.

Grandchild: I make good observations sometimes.

Grandpa: You'll make more when you get older.

Grandchild: I think I'm getting your message about the wisdom of old age.

Grandpa: Another good observation.

Grandchild: OK, enough of your wisdom. You haven't yet told me what it means to have a servant heart, so I can figure out if I have one.

Grandpa: It is a little difficult to define, and it is probably not something you can suddenly acquire. Some people, I think, are born with it, and they exhibit it as they go through life.

Grandchild: So, I can't just decide to have a servant heart?

Grandpa: Probably not.

Grandchild: Are you ever going to tell me what it means?

Grandpa: I will give you my simple definition. Someone with a servant heart anticipates the needs of other people and tries to fill those needs without being asked. They have a special desire to serve others, not because they have been asked but because they want to.

Grandchild: Are they better than other people?

Grandpa: Not better, just different.

Grandchild: Do you have a servant heart?

Grandpa: Not really. I think I have a generous nature, but I would not consider myself as having a servant heart. What about you?

Grandchild: I'm still thinking about it. Who do you think has a servant heart?

Grandpa: I think nurses, social workers and care-givers often have servant hearts, and that is probably a major reason they choose those professions. I think some of my children and grandchildren have servant hearts. You would probably agree with my choices, but I won't name them for fear of hurting someone's feelings.

Grandchild: There you go again, trying to be diplomatic.

Grandpa: I may need help in my old age, so I want my relatives to like me. There are, however, two downsides to having a servant heart.

Grandchild: What are those?

Grandpa: People with servant hearts are usually more sensitive to criticism. When they are criticized, they interpret this to mean they have not met someone else's need. They consider this a failure, and it impacts them more than it would for the rest of us.

Grandchild: What's the other downside?

Grandpa: They can be more easily taken advantage of. This sometimes can result in a difficult marriage, if they marry someone who takes advantage of their desire to serve.

Grandchild: OK, I just decided that I don't have a servant heart because I want a happy marriage.

Grandpa:	That's not the way to insure a happy marriage. There are many other requirements to producing matrimonial bliss. Don't choose your mate simply because he does or does not have a servant heart.
Grandchild:	OK, Grandpa, I think I get the message – or the messages. Thanks.

SPORTS

Grandchild: Grandpa, were you an athlete?
Grandpa: That depends on what you mean by an athlete.
Grandchild: Did you play sports?
Grandpa: Oh yes, I played quite a few different sports.
Grandchild: Were you good?
Grandpa: Not really, but I enjoyed playing.
Grandchild: Did you play football?
Grandpa: Yes, I played in both high school and college.
Grandchild: Did you score any touchdowns?
Grandpa: I scored three in college.
Grandchild: That's not very many.
Grandpa: You're right, but one of them was very important.
Grandchild: Why was that?
Grandpa: It was against our biggest rival, and it was the only touchdown scored in that game. I also blocked a punt for a safety in that game, and we won 8 – 0. It was the only time we beat that team during the four years I was there
Grandchild: So you won the game.
Grandpa: No, I scored the points, but the team won the game. Always remember that in team sports, the success of the team is more important than your individual achievements.
Grandchild: But I want to be the star.

Grandpa:	Then remember that a star only shines against the background of a good team
Grandchild:	Are you trying to give me some advice?
Grandpa:	Only if you are willing to listen. Life has many lessons. I'm just trying to share a few.
Grandchild:	What was your favorite sport?
Grandpa:	Whatever sport was in season. In those days we didn't play each sport all year round. We played a sport during that sport's season, and then we went on to the next sport. It seems that today you have to concentrate on one sport all year long in order to make the team. I think that's unfortunate.
Grandchild:	Why?
Grandpa:	Because it reduces your opportunity to experience other sports and makes excelling at your chosen sport almost a year round job. Since very few people will ever earn a living as an athlete, for most of us, participation in sports is a form of recreation. Why not enjoy a variety of sports.
Grandchild:	So why did you like sports?
Grandpa:	I can think of at least four reasons.
Grandchild:	What are those?
Grandpa:	First of all, sports were fun to play Secondly, I enjoyed competing – trying to see if I could be better at something than someone else. Thirdly, being an athlete produced a level of recognition and acceptance among my peers. Fourthly, sports taught me the value of working together with others to achieve goals. We didn't always succeed, but we pursued these goals as a team. I think this is an important lesson for life.
Grandchild:	Is that another piece of advice.
Grandpa:	If you see it as such.
Grandchild:	What was your least favorite sport?
Grandpa:	Boxing.
Grandchild:	You were a boxer!?

Grandpa: Not really. I had a very short career, but I might impress you by telling you that I won twice as many fights as I lost.

Grandchild: How many fights did you have?

Grandpa: Only three, and I won two of them.

Grandchild: That doesn't sound like a bad record.

Grandpa: Except that the one I lost was by a knockout, and I was unconscious for a half hour.

Grandchild: Is that why you don't like boxing.

Grandpa: It's why I never boxed again, but I don't like boxing because the goal is to render your opponent unconscious. I don't think that's a very noble objective.

Grandchild: So why did you box?

Grandpa: I was in graduate school in Indianapolis and was missing competitive sports. The Golden Gloves boxing tournament was being promoted, and I couldn't resist the temptation to enter. My only previous boxing experience had been occasional skirmishes with my brothers with big gloves to establish the family pecking order. Competing in the Golden Gloves was not one of my wisest decisions. I would not recommend it. However, my brief boxing career did produce the most publicity I ever received in athletics. My picture appeared on the front sports page of the Chicago Tribune before I got knocked out. This was because I was doing social work with young children and was a new father – not because of my prowess as a boxer. The newspaper thought it was a good human interest story, and they believed I might be coming up as the Indianapolis heavyweight champ to compete with champions from other cities in the Chicago Golden Gloves tournament.

Grandchild: I don't think I want to box. .

Grandpa: A very wise decision.

Grandchild: What was your greatest achievement in sports – other than your touchdown against your College rival?

Grandpa: I was not a star in any sport, but I think my most satisfying achievement was in track.

Grandchild: What did you do in track?

Grandpa: I qualified to be a member of a sprint relay team in my senior year of high school.

Grandchild: Doesn't sound very impressive.

Grandpa: It wasn't to others, but it was to me.

Grandchild: Why was that such an achievement?

Grandpa: Because, as a freshman, I was one of the slowest runners in my class. I had big feet, and was certainly not a sprinter.

Grandchild: So, how did you qualify for a sprint relay team?

Grandpa: I usually ran the half mile, because I was too slow for the shorter distances and didn't have enough endurance for the longer races. The half mile is the in-between race – too long for sprinters and too short for distance runners. I wasn't even the best on our team in that event. The last meet of the year was the Conference Championships, and it was decided that only one person from each team could compete in each event. This eliminated my opportunity to compete in any individual event. Our coach felt especially bad for us seniors who weren't going to be able to compete in the last meet of our high school careers, so he had try-outs for the relay teams, in hopes that some of us might qualify. Miraculously, I managed to qualify as the fourth (and slowest) member of our half mile relay team. The coach was delighted, and so was I. We didn't win that race, but I still consider qualifying for a sprint relay team in my senior year of high school as my most significant and unlikely athletic achievement. The beauty of track is that, in addition to competing against opponents, you also compete against yourself. Success can be achieved by improving on your own previous best performances. I consider this another important lesson for life. Always try to do better than you did before. Your future boss will certainly appreciate this.

Grandchild: Another bit of wisdom. Thanks, Grandpa.

SUMMER CAMP

Grandchild: Grandpa, did you ever go to a summer camp when you were a kid?

Grandpa: Oh yes. I started when I was eight years old and for the next eight years I spent two weeks each summer at Phantom Lake YMCA camp in Wisconsin. Most of the fondest and lasting memories of my youth are related to those two weeks.

Grandchild: What did you do that was so memorable?

Grandpa: That camp was where I learned to swim, do crafts, hike, paddle a canoe, sing songs after meals, go on scavenger and treasure hunts and listen to ghost stories around the campfire at night. We also played a game called "Spy".

Grandchild: How did that game work?

Grandpa: Well, a few campers were selected as spies, but their identities were not known by the other campers – even the other spies. The spies would scatter about the campgrounds and then they would try to reach the lodge without being caught. They carried a piece of paper somewhere on their person which stated that they were spies. It might be in their pocket, their shoe or some other good hiding place. If they succeeded in reaching the lodge without being discovered, they would earn points for the spy team. If they were caught and the spy paper found, their team would lose points. The spies would use ingenious methods to avoid being caught – often pretending to be looking for spies

ASK GRANDPA

	while they worked their way closer to the lodge. Sometimes the spies would win and sometimes the campers would win, but it was always great fun.
Grandchild:	I think I would like to be a spy. What other games did you play?
Grandpa:	One of our all-time favorites each year was "Capture the Flag".
Grandchild:	How did that one work?
Grandpa:	The campers were divided into two teams, and each team had a flag which was placed in a circle. The circles were about 50 yards apart and each team tried to steal the other team's flag and bring it back to their own circle. The first team that had both flags in their circle was the winner. The difficulty was that if you were tagged in the other team's territory, you became a prisoner and were put in the other team's circle. The only way you could be freed would be if one of your teammates made it to the circle un-tagged and tagged you. Needless to say, we slept well after we played that game.
Grandchild:	I think I would like to go to camp.
Grandpa:	I would recommend it, but not just for the fun and games. At most camps, you live in cabins with eight or ten other campers and a counselor, and you learn to get along with other people. It is good preparation for the relationships you will develop during the rest of your life. Also, you learn to take care of your living quarters. Beds must be made, clothes hung up and the floor swept every day. At my camp, we had cabin inspections each day, and the neatest cabin would be recognized at the evening meal and a flag placed in front of the winning cabin acknowledging the recognition. .We had a very clean camp, and it was good training for becoming responsible.
Grandchild:	I think this is the "lesson for life" part of our talk. Somehow, you always seem to include that when we talk about anything.

Grandpa:	I have lived a lot of life, so that gives me the right to share what I have learned.
Grandchild:	OK, grandpa, I'll listen. You seem to remember a lot about those two weeks each Summer.
Grandpa:	More than the other 50 weeks in the year. I think, perhaps, it was because I was on my own during those two weeks, and I had to establish my own identity away from my family. I still consider becoming a knight at camp as one of my proudest childhood achievements.
Grandchild:	How did you become a knight?
Grandpa:	Each year, the camp staff would select several campers for knighthood. It was quite an honor. Their identities would always be kept secret until the last night of camp. After everyone had gone to bed that night, the campers who were already knights or a staff member would quietly go to the cabins and wake up those who were chosen and lead them by flashlight to a campfire where the ceremony conferring knighthood would take place.
Grandchild:	So one year you were chosen?
Grandpa:	Yes, and I still remember how thrilled I was. I suppose it is something like becoming an Eagle Scout or receiving a promotion at your place of work or being recognized by an organization of which you are a member. Each of these represent a recognition from peers, and that always produces a special feeling because, aside from your family, your peers know you best. You never are too old or too young to appreciate that kind of recognition.
Grandchild:	Is that your pearl of wisdom for me this time?
Grandpa:	You are becoming more perceptive. Just remember that you create your own reputation, and it stays with you for a long time. Your peers will respect you, or not, based on how you behave. This is true wherever you go and whatever you do.
Grandchild:	I think I get the message. Behave myself. Thanks, Grandpa.

SUMMER VACATIONS

Grandchild: Grandpa, did you go on any summer vacations when you were growing up?

Grandpa: I was blessed to have a mother who loved to go camping, and each summer two of my brothers and I would take off with my mother for an extended trip of a month or more to visit different parts of the Country. Our youngest brother, John, was too young to join us, so he stayed home with our aunt. My father hated camping, so he never joined us, and, since my older brother, Judd, was too young to drive, mom had to do all the driving.

Grandchild: Where did you go?

Grandpa: One year we went to the west coast, one year to the east coast and one year we toured Canada.

Grandchild: You must have covered a lot of miles. How did you keep from getting bored, being in a car for that long without cell phones?

Grandpa: Well, first of all our mother would encourage us to enjoy the sights – the cornfields in Iowa, the lizards skittering across the desert in Arizona, the cascading of the waterfalls in the mountain passes, the steep winding roads up the mountains in the Rockies or the thrill of driving through a tree in the redwood forest in California. We viewed New York City from the top of the Empire State Building, watched money being printed in a Philadelphia mint, toured many historical sites in our Nation's Capital, enjoyed a rodeo in Texas, watched Old Faithful erupt in Yellowstone Park and drove across the Golden Gate Bridge in California.

Grandchild: How did you keep from becoming stir-crazy with so many hours in the car?.

Grandpa: We played games while we travelled.

Grandchild: What kind of games?

Grandpa: One of our favorites was "Alphabet". We would try to find the letters of the alphabet on roadside signs as we passed them. We could use only one letter from each sign, and the first one to finish the alphabet was the winner. Signs such as "Junction", "Quaker State", "Texaco" and "School Zone" became valuable signs because "J", "Q", "X" and "Z" were the hardest letters to find. We also played poker, using the numbers and letters on license plates. We did have one advantage over larger families. There were only four of us so we each had a window seat. Mother sometimes joined in the games, but usually she just focused on the driving and was happy we were not causing problems..

Grandchild: Did you have any unusual experiences on vacation?

Grandpa: We had several near tragedies.

Grandchild: What were those?

Grandpa: Two of them occurred on our western trip. Cars were not as efficient in those days, and it was common to have to stop several times on the drive up a steep mountain to allow the radiator and engine to cool off. Low gears, which are seldom needed today, were a necessity when driving up a mountain back then. One day we were driving up a mountain road in the Rockies and had just rounded a curve when we had to stop to cool off the engine. Mother put on the emergency brake, so the car and trailer wouldn't roll backwards over the cliff, but the emergency brake didn't work! In order to keep the car and trailer from rolling backwards, mom had to use the foot brake, and, after a while, her leg muscles tired and her leg began to shake from the exertion. She told us kids to get out of the car in case she couldn't hold down the brake any longer. I'm not sure what she planned to do if she had to let go of the brake, but, fortunately, a bus pulled up and parked behind us so we couldn't roll back. After the engine had cooled sufficiently, mom was able to drive the car and trailer over the top of the hill and get the brakes fixed in the next town.

Grandchild: What was the other scary experience on your Western trip?

Grandpa: Later on the same trip, we had just gone over the top of a hill in the Rockies and were starting down the other side when our trailer hitch broke and we careened toward the drop off on the left side of the road. Just before we reached the edge, the car miraculously veered back the other way and we ended up on the right side of the road with the trailer tipped over on its side behind us. We had a small trailer, and, with the help of several men who stopped their cars behind us, we were able to tip the trailer back up on its wheels. We had just loaded up with groceries, and I still remember opening the door of the trailer to the sight of beds, utensils, sleeping bags, clothes and groceries piled together in a giant heap on the floor of the trailer. The trailer was towed into the next town, which was a very small town with a movie theatre, and we watched a Shirley Temple movie that night while our trailer was being repaired.

Grandchild: Your mother must have been a strong woman.

Grandpa: She sure was, and I still marvel at her courage to take those trips with us and to survive all the challenges without Dad along to help. She was also a wonderful camper, and she had a great sense of humor. She made travelling and camping fun.

Grandchild: What was your other close call?

Grandpa: We were travelling on a road along the St. Lawrence River in the Gaspe' Peninsula of Canada and had stopped for lunch and a little sight-seeing. We three boys wandered off to explore along the shore of the River, and Judd and I decided to climb a cliff that rose up about 100 feet above the river. . We climbed about 75 feet up a rock face and then found no way to make it up the remaining 25 feet to reach the top. We were perched on a narrow rock ledge, and realized that climbing up is easier than climbing down. At the bottom of the cliff were many large rockss and a fall from where we were might be life threatening. Judd decided that the only solution to our predicament was to inch our way across the narrow ledge we were standing on and to reach the trees that would provide a safe way down. He suggested I go first, so he could provide help if I needed it. I thought that was very generous of him but in retrospect I suspect he really wanted me to test the route because there was certainly no way he could help me if I started to fall. Fortunately, we both made it to the trees safely. Brother David was watching us from the bottom of the cliff, and we threatened him with his life if he told Mom what we had done. Later in the day, after we had travelled many miles, we did share our experience with Mom, but we made it sound like an exciting adventure, rather than a foolish life and death escapade.. .

Grandchild: Did you stay in motels or sleep in the trailer when you travelled?

Grandpa: We always stopped at campgrounds and slept in the trailer. If the weather was nice, we would sometimes snuggle in our sleeping bags outside under the stars.

Grandchild: Why do you think your mom was such a wonderful camper?

Grandpa: First of all, she was very well organized. She had a routine when we reached our campsite, and each of us had a job to do. It might consist of preparing the meal, gathering firewood, making up the beds in the trailer or raking the grounds to make our campsite look neater. Mom would visit our new camp neighbors and within an hour after our arrival would have met most of them. She was a people person. I don't think she ever met a person she couldn't talk to. She also had an inflexible rule. We should always leave our campsite in better condition when we left it than when we arrived.

Grandchild: OK, Grandpa, what's your message of wisdom about your camping experience?

Grandpa: I think you are finally understanding my motive in these conversations.

Grandchild: I may not understand, but I know some message is going to be conveyed.

Grandpa: OK, these are the lessons I learned from my summer vacations with Mom. .

Planning is a very important part of making a vacation enjoyable.

This Country contains an unending treasure chest of interesting sights and experiences.

When everyone helps, tasks are completed more quickly. .

Simple activities can be entertaining and enjoyable. You don't need cell phones for entertainment..

Challenges in life will occur and can be overcome but unnecessary risks are unnecessary risks.

Improve your environment when you have the opportunity.

Mother was a remarkable woman.

God does protect us.

Grandchild: That's quite a list of lessons. Thanks, Grandpa

THEATRE

Grandchild: You like plays, don't you Grandpa?
Grandpa: Not all plays. I like plays that are funny or have an uplifting message.
Grandchild: Would you rather be in them or watch them?
Grandpa: Both
Grandchild: What do you mean, "Both"?
Grandpa: Well, I enjoy getting on stage once in a while, but I also like to watch from the audience.
Grandchild: Why did you get interested in plays?
Grandpa: My father introduced me to live theatre when I was quite young. . He was active in the local Drama Club - sometimes as an actor and often as a Director. He also performed with the USO a few times to entertain the troops during World War II. Occasionally, he took me into Chicago to watch a professional production, and that's when I started to enjoy live theatre. I still remember the very first professional show I saw. "Harvey" was a comedy with a six foot imaginary rabbit, and I really enjoyed it.
Grandchild: What do you mean an imaginary rabbit?
Grandpa: Do you ever play "make-believe"?
Grandchild: Oh sure, I sometimes make believe I'm an astronaut or a great athlete.

Grandpa:	Well, theatre is kind of like "make-believe". Good actors sometimes make you believe in things you can't actually see. In "Harvey" you never see the rabbit, but you are convinced that the actor sees it. It's kind of like believing you're an astronaut.
Grandchild:	I like playing make-believe.
Grandpa:	Then you will probably like plays.
Grandchild:	What is your favorite part?
Grandpa:	Whatever part I'm playing at the moment. Sometimes I'm type casted.
Grandchild:	What do you mean type casted?
Grandpa:	Well sometimes people play the parts of characters who are very much like them. For instance, I may play the part of a doctor because I'm a doctor. An athlete may play the part of an athlete or a grumpy man play the part of a grumpy man.
Grandchild:	So then you really don't have to act. You just play yourself.
Grandpa:	Well, you still have to act, but it's a little easier.
Grandchild:	Do you ever play someone who is not like you at all?
Grandpa:	Yes, and those parts can be the most fun – to act like someone totally different. It would be like you pretending to be a great dancer.
Grandchild:	That's not going to happen!
Grandpa:	One of the biggest compliments I ever received from acting was when I had a part where I was a grouchy old man.
Grandchild:	That doesn't sound like you.
Grandpa:	I hope not, but I had to pretend I was. That's why I enjoyed the compliment I received after that performance.
Grandchild:	What was the compliment?
Grandpa:	It wasn't really intended as a compliment. My eight year old granddaughter saw the show and after the show she was very upset.
Grandchild:	Why was she upset?

Grandpa: She told her mother that we needed to tell people that I really was not like that character.

Grandchild: You must have been a convincing grouch.

Grandpa: Apparently so. At least I convinced my granddaughter. What kind of books do you like to read?

Grandchild: I like mysteries and action stories.

Grandpa: And why do you like those?

Grandchild: Because they are exciting, and I want to see what happens.

Grandpa: Plays are kind of like watching a good book being acted out. In fact, some plays were first written as books. In theatre, actors try to convince the audience that what is happening on stage is real. Good actors will even make you feel the emotions they are feeling. They will make you laugh or cry or love the hero and hate the villain. You probably feel that way when you are reading a good book.

Grandchild: Oh yes, I often imagine myself as one of the characters – usually the hero. Did you ever meet any real actors?

Grandpa: Well, actually, anyone who performs is a real actor, but most people don't get paid for acting. They do it because they enjoy it. They might perform in school productions or in a community theatre – or perhaps for some organization that wants some entertainment. If they get paid, they are considered professional actors.

Grandchild: Did you ever get paid for acting?

Grandpa: No, but my father took me backstage once after a show to meet a professional actor. He had also appeared in a few movies. I was impressed that Dad knew him, and it was a thrill to actually meet a professional actor. Actually, I think my father may have had an unfulfilled dream of being a professional actor, but he decided it was not a good way to support a family.

Grandchild: Did you ever want to be a professional actor?

Grandpa: No

Grandchild: Why not?

Grandpa: Actors work very hard rehearsing and performing, and they often have to do a lot of travelling. It is not a very stable life if you want to raise a family. Often times professional actors will do the same show hundreds of times, and, while the audiences change and the applause is rewarding, it wouldt be difficult to maintain the same enthusiasm after that many performances. Amateurs, on the other hand, rehearse a show for six or eight weeks, have a few performances and then are done. It is not a job and doesn't dominate their lives. While I like to believe that at times my performances were as good as a professional's, I had no desire to do it for a living. The applause or laughter of the audience was reward enough for me. .

Grandchild: Did you ever see a musical?

Grandpa: Oh yes. I remember when my father announced that he was taking me to a musical. I was not thrilled. I thought it would be an opera with songs sung in a foreign language by men and women in leotards. Instead, to my delight, we saw "South Pacific", and I decided I liked that kind of musical.

Grandchild: Did you ever have a big part in a play?

Grandpa: If you mean parts that required me to learn lots of lines, yes I had a few, but there is a saying in theatre, attributed to Shakespeare, I think; "There are no small parts, only small actors." Some of the most fun parts are small roles that have very few lines. One of my favorite on stage lines was in a production of "Oklahoma". I was just one of the cowboys, and my only line in the show was after the villain had fallen on his knife. As I bent over him, my line was, "Let's get this man to a real doctor." Only in a small town would this receive the response it did. The line always produced much laughter because I was a family doctor in real life. It was supposed to be a serious scene, but even the other actors had to turn their backs, so the audience would not see them smiling. I made the most of my one line.

Grandchild: Do you think I should get in plays?

Grandpa: Only if it is something you want to do, but if you do, you will learn some of life's valuable lessons.

Grandchild: Like what?

Grandpa: You will learn the importance of preparation. Many hours of rehearsal are required to put on a successful production.

Grandchild: You mean I would have to memorize a bunch of lines.

Grandpa: Yes, but that is only part of preparing for a production. You also need to learn how to move on stage and how best to deliver your lines, so they can be heard clearly by the audience. If you're in s a musical, in addition to singing, you may have to learn to do a little dancing.

Grandchild: I don't like to dance.

Grandpa: In order to be a successful actor, sometimes you will have to do things you may not like to do. This is an important lesson because often times in your life you will be required to do things you really don't want to do. Sometimes, after you learn to do something new, you may find you actually enjoy it. Don't worry; if you are in a show, you will have lots of help from the directors. They want you to do well.

Grandchild: What else will I learn if I am in a play?

Grandpa: You will learn to work together with other people to create a show that people will enjoy. You will also have the thrill of hearing the applause from the audience when you put on a good performance.

Grandchild: What if I forget one of my lines?

Grandpa: There isn't an actor who has lived who hasn't forgotten a line. Stage presence is learning to fill the blank spots with something, so the audience doesn't know you forgot it. One time I missed a whole scene. Not sure what the other

	actors did, but they covered my absence, so the audience didn't even miss me.
Grandchild:	Maybe I will try out for a play. It sounds like fun. But I want to be an athlete, too.
Grandpa:	You can do both, at least while you are in school, but one advantage of theatre is that there are no losers like there are in sports. Everyone on stage or in the audience is a winner.
Grandchild:	You have a point. Thanks Grandpa.

THE OLDEN DAYS

Grandchild: Grandpa, what was it like when you were growing up?
Grandpa: That was a long time ago, but it was after the dinosaurs.
Grandchild: You're funny. Things must have been quite different way back then.
Grandpa: They were different alright.
Grandchild: How did you travel?
Grandpa: Oh, we had cars, but the cars back then didn't have all the fancy conveniences of today's cars. For one thing, we had to learn to shift gears. Most cars didn't have automatic shifting, and most families had only one car, so two car garages were uncommon.
Grandchild: Where did you do your shopping?
Grandpa: We didn't have the big supermarkets you have today, so we did a lot of our grocery shopping at the neighborhood stores. Many of these stores had charge accounts, so you could charge your groceries or your medicines and then pay up at the end of each month.
Grandchild: Kind of like today's credit cards.
Grandpa: Except that it was more personal because each store had its own account. The owners were your neighbors. If you were short of money one month, you could talk to the store owner and work out a payment plan.
Grandchild: And they would trust you?

Grandpa: Trust was part of our culture back then – especially in small towns. We didn't lock our doors, we let our children play outdoors until dark, and business negotiations sometimes required just a verbal agreement and a handshake.

Grandchild: Yeah, today you can't even trust your internet, and people purchase all kinds of gadgets to make them feel safe in their own homes. What else was different back then?

Grandpa: We were much more frugal back then.

Grandchild: What do you mean, frugal?

Grandpa: Well, we had just come through a depression and a World War, so very few people had a lot of money to spend. We had to control our spending more carefully. Most people weren't starving, but what you now call "junk food" wasn't on the family shopping list. Frugal meant that we didn't spend money as freely as people do now. During the War, many people even had victory gardens in their back yards, and my parents raised chickens in their back yard, so we could enjoy meat more often. Meat was rationed during the war.

Grandchild: Did people protest against the War back then?

Grandpa: That was another difference from today. Patriotism was very strong then because we had been attacked by the Japanese, and the Germans were conquering Europe. There were a few who protested before we were attacked, but I don't recall any big protest marches, and most people went into military service willingly.

Grandchild: Were families more stable when you were growing up? Today, a lot of people live together before they get married and I think I heard that nearly 50% of marriages end in divorce.

Grandpa: In my small town, divorce was uncommon and marriage almost always preceded living together. If an unmarried girl got pregnant, she would leave town for a while to stay with an aunt or some other family member and then return after she had the baby.

Grandchild: Now they have baby showers to celebrate the event. Did you have welfare back then?

Grandpa: There were some government programs, but much of welfare in my day was taken care of by churches, family and friends.

Grandchild: Could everyone get medical care back then?

Grandpa: People got medical care, but sometimes, if they couldn't afford to pay for it, it was free, We didn't have a government medical program back then, so if a poor person needed care, most doctors would provide it free or charge much less than their usual fee. When I was in practice, I would sometimes use the barter system and trade my medical services for a dozen eggs or some ears of corn.

Grandchild: Now, the poor people have their medical care paid for by the government.

Grandpa: This means the doctor no longer feels the need to be charitable, which I think is unfortunate.

Grandchild: Can you think of anything else that was different in your day?

Grandpa: I can think of a lot of things, but one of the most important differences is that I think we respected our Country more and had a greater appreciation for the opportunities it provided us. Today, to be honest, I am baffled and disappointed by the many protests that have been occurring. Our Nation is not perfect, but I still think it is the best place in the World to live, and I feel blessed to have been born here. I hope you feel the same way.

Grandchild: I do, even if it is not the same as when you were growing up. Thanks for sharing, Grandpa

TOLERANCE

Grandchild: Are you a tolerant person, Grandpa?
Grandpa: That depends on what you mean by tolerant.
Grandchild: I mean do you tolerate other people's opinions.
Grandpa: Sometimes.
Grandchild: What do you mean, sometimes?
Grandpa: Let me ask you a question.
Grandchild: I thought I was asking the questions.
Grandpa: Sometimes you learn more by answering questions.
Grandchild: I think you are about to lead me into one of your logic traps.
Grandpa: Perhaps, but I want to find out if you have limits to your tolerance.
Grandchild: Not sure what you mean, but let's have your question.
Grandpa: If someone stole something from you, would you tolerate it?
Grandchild: No! Stealing is a crime.
Grandpa: Suppose the thief has a starving family, he doesn't steal very much and he is just trying to feed his family.
Grandchild: I might be more tolerant then.
Grandpa: Suppose you love to sing and you want to be in a musical, but you find out at the auditions that you would have to use profanity on stage. Would you still audition?
Grandchild: I really like to sing, but I don't like to swear, so I probably would choose not to be in that show.

Grandpa: Suppose only someone else in the cast would have to use profanity.

Grandchild: Then I might consider auditioning, because I wouldn't have to compromise my values.

Grandpa: Suppose a friend of yours invites you to join him in breaking the windows in someone's house.

Grandchild: I couldn't do that. That would be wrong.

Grandpa: What if the windows were the only ones not broken in a dilapidated, abandoned, unoccupied shed out in the country.

Grandchild: I might be tempted to join him.

Grandpa: It sound like sometimes you are tolerant and sometimes you aren't.

Grandchild: I guess so.

Grandpa: Don't worry. We all are, and that doesn't make our lack of tolerance bad.

Grandchild: So, what makes our tolerance good sometimes and not so good at other times?

Grandpa: Our values. We all have a moral compass that controls our thoughts and our actions. We don't all agree on what that compass tells us, but I suspect even evildoers know that what they are doing is wrong.

Grandchild: So, it's ok if I am not tolerant of things that go against my values?

Grandpa: Not only is it ok, but you will also be sending a message to others that you feel certain behaviors are wrong.

Grandchild: How do I know what to tolerate and what to not tolerate?

Grandpa: Think of it this way. You possess an imaginary value balance scale. Tolerance is on one side of the scale, and your values are on the other side. The more you value something, the less tolerant you are of things that go against that value. If an action or behavior is not something that has much value for you, you are more apt to tolerate it.

Grandchild: Does everyone use the same scale?

Grandpa: Unfortunately not. Even two people who believe in the Ten Commandments don't always agree on their meaning. Someone might criticize me for being intolerant of something they think is unimportant, but that I place great value on. For me, the Sanctity of life has great value, but someone else might consider me intolerant if I oppose abortion. We don't all use the same value scale, which is why we have disagreements. A thief is obviously using a different value scale than most of us use to justify his actions.

Grandchild: If I tolerate someone's behavior, does that mean I have to agree with him?

Grandpa: Excellent question. Tolerance and acceptance are two different things.

Grandchild: What do you mean?

Grandpa: You might think that having to pay taxes on the property you own is wrong, but you can be tolerant of someone who thinks that property taxes are necessary. This doesn't mean you agree with that person, but you tolerate their different opinion.

Grandchild: Why can't we just be tolerant of everybody?

Grandpa: You mean, not be critical of anything people do? Total freedom has a pleasant ring to it, and it has a name. It is called Anarchy.

Grandchild: What is Anarchy? You shouldn't use words I don't understand.

Grandpa: You should understand the words I use. Anarchy is total individual freedom without any outside controls. In other words, everyone is free to do whatever he or she wants. The only limits are those that each individual chooses to impose on himself or herself.

Grandchild: Sounds like total chaos.

Grandpa: Exactly. You figured that out quickly. I'm impressed.

Grandchild: Don't be because, as usual, you always find a way to tie me in knots with your logic. I'm not even sure how we got to anarchy from tolerance.
Grandpa: I'm sure that, in time, the logic will descend on you.
Grandchild: If you say so. I'm not even sure I should thank you for this discussion.
Grandpa: One of your values should be to respect your elders.
Grandchild: Perhaps that value isn't very heavy on my scale.
Grandpa: But it's heavy on mine.
Grandchild: OK, but you said I can be tolerant without agreeing. Thanks, Grandpa.

VOLUNTEERING

Grandchild: Grandpa, you do a lot of volunteering, don't you?
Grandpa: Not compared to a lot of other people.
Grandchild: Why do people volunteer?
Grandpa: That is a rather profound question.
Grandchild: You mean I am profound?
Grandpa: No, the question is profound. You are not old enough to be profound.
Grandchild: OK, so why do people volunteer?
Grandpa: People volunteer for different reasons. People may feel very strongly about an issue or a cause, and they volunteer their time to support their convictions. Some people might feel strongly that everyone should have a decent place to live, so they volunteer their time and talent to Habitat For Humanity. Former President Jimmy Carter is in his 90's and still does this. Other people feel strongly that women with unplanned pregnancies need support, so they volunteer at Crisis Pregnancy Centers. Others volunteer in soup kitchens to help feed the hungry.
Grandchild: Do people get paid when they volunteer?
Grandpa: Not usually.
Grandchild: They offer to help, knowing that they won't get paid?
Grandpa: Sometimes they are even disappointed when they are offered payment for what they have done.

Grandchild:	Why would they be disappointed? I would think they would be thrilled.
Grandpa:	Because, if you get paid, it takes away some of the pleasure of doing good. You feel better if you do something simply because you want to help, without expecting anything in return.
Grandchild:	Not sure I understand that logic.
Grandpa:	You're probably too young to completely understand, but let me try to make it a little simpler.
Grandchild:	I like simple things.
Grandpa:	Suppose after dinner tonight, you decide to be more generous than usual and offer to do the dishes without being asked.
Grandchild:	Not very likely, but my mother would be thrilled.- and probably shocked.
Grandpa:	And how would you feel?
Grandchild:	I guess I would feel I was cementing my status as my parent's favorite child.
Grandpa:	Suppose you did the dishes after your mother asked you?
Grandchild:	I would probably complain before I did them.
Grandpa:	In the first instance you were volunteering; in the second you were obeying a request.
Grandchild:	I think you are trying to send me a message with this example.
Grandpa:	Very perceptive. Most people volunteer because it makes them feel better than they would if they did something after they were asked, or if they were getting paid for what they did.
Grandchild:	So, volunteering is good?
Grandpa:	I think you got the message.
Grandchild:	It will take a while to sink in. Not sure I'm quite ready to do the dishes tonight. Thanks, Grandpa. .

WAR

Grandchild: Grandpa, do you like war?
Grandpa: I don't think many people like war.
Grandchild: Then why do we have wars?
Grandpa: Let me ask you a question. If someone broke into your house, tried to steal your possessions and intended to hurt your baby sister and your mother, how would you feel?
Grandchild: I would be very angry.
Grandpa: And what would you do?
Grandchild: I would try to stop him.
Grandpa: How would you do that?
Grandchild: I would tell him to get out of the house and leave us alone.
Grandpa: And suppose he refused to leave.
Grandchild: I would call the police.
Grandpa: Do you really think he would let you call the police.
Grandchild: Probably not.
Grandpa: Then what would you do?
Grandchild: I would hope my father would get him to leave.
Grandpa: And how would your father do that?
Grandchild: He might throw him out. My father is pretty strong.
Grandpa: Suppose the intruder had a gun and was threatening to kill you.
Grandchild: Hopefully, my father would have his gun.
Grandpa: And suppose your father shot the intruder before he could shoot you.

Grandchild:	It was his fault he got shot. He shouldn't have been in our house.
Grandpa:	So you are in favor of war.
Grandchild:	I'm in favor of self-defense and protecting what is mine.
Grandpa:	That's what war is, only on a much larger scale. If one Country wants to take the possessions of another Country and peaceful means don't stop them, the other Country may fight back, and we have a war.
Grandchild:	Why can't Countries just keep what is theirs? Why do they have to take things from other Countries?
Grandpa:	If we could answer that question, we could have lasting peace. Unfortunately, some Countries have rulers who are not satisfied with what they have. They want more. Strong Nations try to conquer weak Nations, so they can take over their possessions. That's why Nations have armies – to protect themselves against other Nations.
Grandchild:	Why did our Country go to war?
Grandpa:	We were trying to protect what we had. We did not go to war to gain more possessions. Germany and Japan, on the other hand, wanted control of more territory.
Grandchild:	Why did we care what happened in Europe or Japan? They were not our Country.
Grandpa:	We were like your father. We wanted to help protect our friends. The Countries that Germany conquered during the two World Wars were our friends, so we went to their aid. If we hadn't helped them, all of Europe would probably have been conquered and then Germany might have crossed the ocean and attacked us. Against the possible intruder in your home, your father would protect his family, but he would also be protecting himself.
Grandchild:	So, I guess sometimes wars are necessary.
Grandpa:	Yes, even though we would prefer to use peaceful methods. Sometimes wars are necessary to protect our possessions and our freedoms, but I hope you never have to fight in one.
Grandchild:	I hope so, too. Thanks Grandpa.

WEATHER

Grandchild: Grandpa, do you remember any really bad weather?
Grandpa: I have a few notable memories.
Grandchild: Like what?
Grandpa: Well, I remember when I was doing my medical internship in Saginaw, Michigan, and we had a major two foot snowstorm that essentially shut down the city. I lived across the street from the hospital where I was interning, so I was able to walk to work, but it was a problem for hospital employees to get to work.
Grandchild: So, what did they do? They certainly had to have nurses to take care of the patients.
Grandpa: They put out an appeal for people with snowmobiles to pick up the nurses and bring them to work.
Grandchild: Did they get many volunteers?
Grandpa: More than they could use. It seems like the macho snowmobile owners were delighted to transport pretty nurses to the hospital on their machines. The hospital had a full staff.
Grandchild: Any other weather memories?
Grandpa: One Christmas, the Chicago area had enough snow that there were large piles around the houses. A couple of my nephews decided it would be great fun to jump off the front porch roof into the snow pile in front. Unfortunately,

	one of them discovered that the snow was not as soft as he anticipated, and he broke his leg in the process.
Grandchild:	Doesn't sound like a very merry Christmas for him.
Grandpa:	Not really, but I suppose it was one of life lessons learned.
Grandchild:	Did you ever have to travel very far during a big snow storm?
Grandpa:	One time, when we were building our Amway business, we travelled to Dover, Delaware from Michigan in a big storm. What normally was a six hour trip in good weather turned into a ten hour white knuckle challenge, but we were committed to our business-building goals, so we were proud of our accomplishment of reaching our destination in spite of the weather. Unfortunately, the people we travelled to see weren't nearly as interested in our goals, so, even though they lived only two blocks away, they chose not to attend our scheduled meeting. .
Grandchild:	You travelled that far to see one person?
Grandpa:	Sometimes the pursuit of a goal overcomes logical thinking. Another time, when we were travelling home from Grand Rapids in a heavy snowstorm we were a little wiser. We pulled off the highway and spent the night in a motel.
Grandchild:	Why do you choose to continue to live in a location that gets so cold? Why don't you move south where it's warmer?
Grandpa:	Because then we wouldn't appreciate Spring so much.
Grandchild:	Not sure that qualifies as a logical answer, but thanks anyway, Grandpa.

WHEN A LOVED ONE DIES

Grandchild: Grandpa, you must be really sad that Grandma has passed away.
Grandpa: I do miss her, but I would not say I am sad.
Grandchild: What do you mean?
Grandpa: You know, we did spend 68 years together!
Grandchild: Yes, but now she is gone.
Grandpa: We don't see her now, but I would not say she is gone. I remember her every day. When I sit in the recliner couch we used to share; when I eat a meal and remember the many meals she prepared for me; when I attend an event and remember the events we attended together; when I share time with friends we used to share times with; even when I do the laundry or dishes and remember her instructions in how to do it correctly. No, she is not really gone. Besides, she had the most beautiful last week of life anyone could wish for.
Grandchild: In what way?
Grandpa: She died at home, in no pain, surrounded by family and mentally alert until the end. In fact, near the end when she could no longer talk, she was still expressing her opinion with nods of her head.
Grandchild: So, you are doing ok?
Grandpa: I have my moments, but, yes, I am doing ok. I recently heard a profound comment from a priest at the funeral

of a nineteen year old boy, who had died unexpectedly. The priest said, "We have a tendency to be angry and upset when someone that young dies – even angry and upset at God. Perhaps we are asking the wrong question. Perhaps the question should not be 'Why did he die?' but 'Why did he live?'"

After the service, the distraught mother also made a meaningful comment when she remarked, "I am not angry with God for taking my son at such a young age. I am thankful to God for giving me 19 years with my son."

I have no regrets. I am thankful for the 68 years your Grandma and I had together, and I take consolation in the belief that she is in a better place, free of infirmities and the burdens of life. She was a woman of a very strong faith, and now I must maintain that faith until it is time for me to join her once again.

Grandchild: Thanks, Grandpa. I love you.

WORLD WAR II

Grandchild: Grandpa, were you ever a soldier?
Grandpa: I was a sailor. I was in the Navy.
Grandchild: When was that?
Grandpa: At the end of the Second World War.
Grandchild: Wow! That was a long time ago.
Grandpa: It sure was – way back in 1944. Remember, I'm pretty old.
Grandchild: Why did you join the Navy?
Grandpa: I felt I would be safer on a ship than in a foxhole. In those days most every young man went into military service. If you didn't join voluntarily, you were drafted.
Grandchild: What do you mean –"drafted".
Grandpa: Well, we needed a big Army and Navy because we were fighting two wars, one against Germany and one against Japan. So the government passed a law that if you were a healthy young man, at least 18 years old, you were required to spend time serving your Country in our armed forces.
Grandchild: So you didn't have a choice.
Grandpa: Not really, but since everyone had the same obligation, we didn't think we were being asked to do anything special. In fact, some young men who couldn't pass the physical, felt guilty because they couldn't serve their Country. Patriotism was very high then because our Nation had been attacked in Pearl Harbor by the Japanese.

Grandchild: How long were you in the Navy?
Grandpa: Only two years.
Grandchild: We won that war, didn't we.
Grandpa: Yes, but we sacrificed a lot of American lives to do so. I think sometimes people today forget the sacrifices that were made, so that we can have the freedom we enjoy today.
Grandchild: Did you ever get shot?
Grandpa: No. I was fortunate.
Grandchild: I don't like war because people always get killed. Why do we have wars anyway?
Grandpa: I don't think many people like war, but sometimes wars are necessary in order to protect our freedoms. World War II was that kind of war. If America hadn't fought in that war, all of Europe would have been controlled by Hitler.
Grandchild: Who was Hitler?
Grandpa: He was an evil German Dictator who wanted to control the world. He killed and imprisoned hundreds of thousands of Jews and other people he didn't like. His powerful army conquered most of Europe. Only England remained, and he would have conquered England if we had not gotten involved when we did.
Grandchild: Why did we care what happened in Europe?
Grandpa: That's a question many Americans were asking at that time.
Grandchild: So, why did we get involved?
Grandpa: Because our Country was attacked when Pearl Harbor was bombed.
Grandchild: But that was by the Japanese. What did that have to do with Europe?
Grandpa: The Germans and the Japanese were allies, and they both wanted conquests. If the Germans weren't stopped before they defeated England, they might have crossed the Atlantic, and we would have been fighting them on

	our shores. And the Japanese had already attacked us in Hawaii. After the attack on Pearl Harbor, there was no longer much resistance to our entering the war.
Grandchild:	I'm glad we won that war. I guess I should be more grateful for the men who fought for our freedom.
Grandpa:	Actually, it was not only men. The women did a lot, too. Some of them served in the armed forces, and many of them worked in the factories that produced tanks and airplanes. Most everyone was involved in the war effort in some capacity.
Grandchild:	I hope we don't have to fight another war.
Grandpa:	I hope so, too, but, if we do, I hope that your generation will respond with the same effort and patriotism that ours did.
Grandchild:	Thanks, Grandpa.

CPSIA information can be obtained
at www.ICGtesting.com
Printed in the USA
FSHW021139040620
70866FS